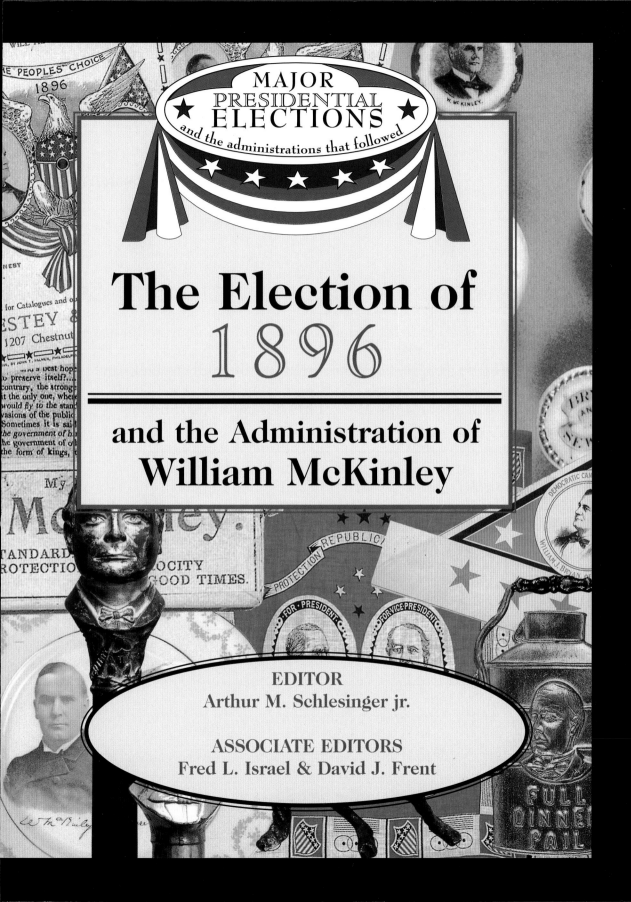

MAJOR PRESIDENTIAL ELECTIONS
and the administrations that followed

The Election of
1896

and the Administration of
William McKinley

EDITOR
Arthur M. Schlesinger jr.

ASSOCIATE EDITORS
Fred L. Israel & David J. Frent

The Elections of 1789 & 1792 and the Administration of George Washington

The Election of 1800 and the Administration of Thomas Jefferson

The Election of 1828 and the Administration of Andrew Jackson

The Election of 1840 and the Harrison/Tyler Administrations

The Election of 1860 and the Administration of Abraham Lincoln

The Election of 1876 and the Administration of Rutherford B. Hayes

The Election of 1896 and the Administration of William McKinley

The Election of 1912 and the Administration of Woodrow Wilson

The Election of 1932 and the Administration of Franklin D. Roosevelt

The Election of 1948 and the Administration of Harry S. Truman

The Election of 1960 and the Administration of John F. Kennedy

The Election of 1968 and the Administration of Richard Nixon

The Election of 1976 and the Administration of Jimmy Carter

The Election of 1980 and the Administration of Ronald Reagan

The Election of 2000 and the Administration of George W. Bush

The Election of
1896

and the Administration of William McKinley

EDITOR

Arthur M. Schlesinger, jr.
Albert Schweitzer Chair in the Humanities
The City University of New York

★

ASSOCIATE EDITORS

Fred L. Israel
Department of History
The City College of New York

David J. Frent
The David J. and Janice L. Frent
Political Americana Collection

Mason Crest Publishers
Philadelphia

Produced by OTTN Publishing, Stockton, New Jersey

Mason Crest Publishers
370 Reed Road
Broomall PA 19008
www.masoncrest.com

Research Consultant: Patrick R. Hilferty
Editorial Assistant: Jane Ziff

First printing

1 3 5 7 9 8 6 4 2

Library of Congress Cataloging-in-Publication Data

The election of 1896 and the administration of William McKinley / editor, Arthur M. Schlesinger,
Jr.; associate editors, Fred L. Israel & David J. Frent.
  p. cm. — (Major presidential elections and the administrations that followed)
Summary: A discussion of the presidential election of 1896 and the subsequent administration of
William McKinley, based on source documents.
 Includes bibliographical references and index.
 ISBN 1-59084-357-6
1. Presidents—United States—Election—1896—Juvenile literature. 2. Presidents—United
States—Election—1896—Sources—Juvenile literature. 3. McKinley, William, 1843-1901—Juvenile
literature. 4. United States—Politics and government—1897-1901—Juvenile literature. 5. United
States—Politics and government—1897-1901—Sources—Juvenile literature. [1. Presidents—
Election—1896. 2. Elections. 3. McKinley, William, 1843-1901. 4. United States—Politics and
government—1897-1901.]
I. Schlesinger, Arthur Meier, 1917- . II. Israel, Fred L. III. Frent, David J. IV. Series.
E710 .E43 2002
973.8'8—dc21

2002011263

★ **Publisher's note: all quotations in this book come from original sources, and contain the spelling and grammatical inconsistencies of the original text.** ★

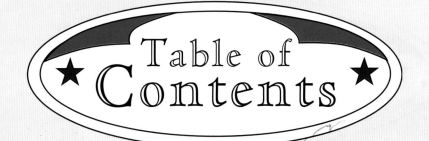

Table of Contents

America suffers from a sort of intermittent fever—what one may call a quintan ague. Every fourth year there come terrible shakings, passing into the hot fit of the presidential election; then follows what physicians call "the interval"; then again the fit.

—James Bryce, *The American Commonwealth* (1888)

Running for president is the central rite in the American political order. It was not always so. *Choosing* the chief magistrate had been the point of the quadrennial election from the beginning, but it took a long while for candidates to *run* for the highest office in the land; that is, to solicit, visibly and actively, the support of the voters. These volumes show through text and illustration how those aspiring to the White House have moved on from ascetic self-restraint to shameless self-merchandising. This work thereby illuminates the changing ways the American people have conceived the role of their President. I hope it will also recall to new generations some of the more picturesque and endearing dimensions of American politics.

The primary force behind the revolution in campaign attitudes and techniques was a development unforeseen by the men who framed the Constitution—the rise of the party system. Party competition was not at all their original intent. Quite the contrary: inspired at one or two removes by Lord Bolingbroke's British tract of half a century earlier, *The Idea of a Patriot King*, the Founding Fathers envisaged a Patriot President, standing above party and faction, representing the whole people, offering the nation non-partisan leadership virtuously dedicated to the common good.

The ideal of the Patriot President was endangered, the Founding Fathers believed, by twin menaces—factionalism and factionalism's ugly offspring, the demagogue. Party competition would only encourage unscrupulous men to appeal to popular passion and prejudice. Alexander Hamilton in the 71st Federalist bemoaned the plight of the people, "beset as they continually are . . . by the snares of the ambitious, the avaricious, the desperate, by the artifices of men who possess their confidence more than they deserve it, and of those who seek to possess rather than to deserve it."

Pervading the Federalist was a theme sounded explicitly both in the first paper and the last: the fear that unleashing popular passions would bring on "the military despotism of a victorious demagogue." If the "mischiefs of faction" were, James Madison admitted in the Tenth Federalist, "sown in the nature of man," the object of politics was to repress this insidious disposition, not to yield to it. "If I could not go to heaven but with a party," said Thomas Jefferson, "I would not go there at all."

So the Father of his Country in his Farewell Address solemnly warned his countrymen against "the baneful effects of the spirit of party." That spirit, Washington conceded, was "inseparable from our nature"; but for popular government it was "truly their worst enemy." The "alternate domination of one faction over another," Washington said, would lead in the end to "formal and permanent despotism." The spirit of a party, "a fire not to be quenched . . . demands a uniform vigilance to prevent its bursting into a flame, lest, instead of warming, it should consume."

Yet even as Washington called on Americans to "discourage and restrain" the spirit of party, parties were beginning to crystallize around him. The eruption of partisanship in defiance of such august counsel argued that party competition might well serve functional necessities in the democratic republic.

After all, honest disagreement over policy and principle called for candid debate. And parties, it appeared, had vital roles to play in the consummation of the Constitution. The distribution of powers among three equal branches inclined the national government toward a chronic condition of stalemate. Parties offered the means of overcoming the constitutional separation of powers by coordinating the executive and legislative branches and furnishing the connective tissue essential to effective government. As national associations, moreover, parties were a force against provincialism and separatism. As instruments of compromise, they encouraged, within the parties as well as between them, the containment and mediation of national quarrels, at least until slavery broke the parties up. Henry D. Thoreau cared little enough for politics, but he saw the point: "Politics is, as it were, the gizzard of society, full of grit and gravel, and the two political parties are its two opposite halves, which grind on each other."

Furthermore, as the illustrations in these volumes so gloriously remind us, party competition was a great source of entertainment and fun—all the more important in those faraway days before the advent of baseball and football, of movies and radio and television. "To take a hand in the regulation of society and to discuss it," Alexis de Tocqueville observed when he visited America in the 1830s, "is his biggest concern and, so to speak, the only pleasure an American knows. . . . Even the women frequently attend public meetings and listen to political harangues as a recreation from their household labors. Debating clubs are, to a certain extent, a substitute for theatrical entertainments."

Condemned by the Founding Fathers, unknown to the Constitution, parties nonetheless imperiously forced themselves into political life. But the party system rose from the bottom up. For half a century, the first half-dozen Presidents continued to hold themselves above party. The disappearance of the Federalist Party after the War of 1812 suspended party competition. James Monroe, with no opponent at all in the election of 1820, presided proudly over the Era of Good Feelings, so called because there were no parties around to excite ill feelings. Monroe's successor, John Quincy Adams, despised electioneering and inveighed against the "fashion of peddling for popularity by traveling around the country gathering crowds together, hawking for public dinners, and spouting empty speeches." Men of the old republic believed presidential candidates should be men who already deserved the people's confidence rather than those seeking to win it. Character and virtue, not charisma and ambition, should be the grounds for choosing a President.

Adams was the last of the old school. Andrew Jackson, by beating him in the 1828 election, legitimized party politics and opened a new political era. The rationale of the new school was provided by Jackson's counselor and successor, Martin Van Buren, the classic philosopher of the role of party in the American democracy. By the time Van Buren took his own oath of office in 1837, parties were entrenched as the instruments of American self-government. In Van Buren's words, party battles "rouse the sluggish to exertion, give increased energy to the most active intellect, excite a salutary vigilance over our public functionaries, and prevent that apathy which has proved the ruin of Republics."

Apathy may indeed have proved the ruin of republics, but rousing the sluggish to exertion proved, ironically, the ruin of Van Buren. The architect of the party system became the first casualty of the razzle-dazzle campaigning the system quickly generated. The Whigs' Tippecanoe-and-Tyler-too campaign of 1840 transmuted the democratic Van Buren into a gilded aristocrat and assured his defeat at the polls. The "peddling for popularity" John Quincy Adams had deplored now became standard for party campaigners.

But the new methods were still forbidden to the presidential candidates themselves. The feeling lingered from earlier days that stumping the country in search of votes was demagoguery beneath the dignity of the presidency. Van Buren's code permitted—indeed expected—parties to inscribe their creed in platforms and candidates to declare their principles in letters published in newspapers. Occasionally candidates—William Henry Harrison in 1840, Winfield Scott in 1852—made a speech, but party surrogates did most of the hard work.

As late as 1858, Van Buren, advising his son John, one of the great popular orators of the time, on the best way to make it to the White House, emphasized the "rule . . . that the people will never make a man President who is so importunate as to show by his life and conversation that he not only has an eye on, but is in active pursuit of the office. . . . No man who has laid himself out for it, and was unwise enough to let the people into his secret, ever yet obtained it. Clay, Calhoun, Webster, Scott, and a host of lesser lights, should serve as a guide-post to future aspirants."

The continuing constraint on personal campaigning by candidates was reinforced by the desire of party managers to present their nominees as all things to all men. In 1835 Nicholas Biddle, the wealthy Philadelphian who had been Jackson's mortal opponent in the famous Bank War, advised the Whigs not to let General Harrison "say one single word about his principles or his creed. . . . Let him say nothing, promise nothing. Let no committee, no convention, no town meeting ever extract from him a single word about what he thinks now, or what he will do hereafter. Let the use of pen and ink be wholly forbidden as if he were a mad poet in Bedlam."

We cherish the memory of the famous debates in 1858 between Abraham Lincoln and Stephen A. Douglas. But those debates were not part of a presidential election. When the presidency was at stake two years later, Lincoln gave no campaign speeches on the issues darkly dividing the country. He even expressed doubt about party platforms—"the formal written platform system," as he called it. The candidate's character and record, Lincoln thought, should constitute his platform: "On just such platforms all our earlier and better Presidents were elected."

However, Douglas, Lincoln's leading opponent in 1860, foreshadowed the future when he broke the sound barrier and dared venture forth on thinly disguised campaign tours. Yet Douglas established no immediate precedent. Indeed, half a dozen years later Lincoln's successor, Andrew Johnson, discredited presidential stumping by his "swing around the circle" in the midterm election of 1866. "His performances in a western tour in advocacy of his own election," commented Benjamin F. Butler, who later led the fight in Congress for Johnson's impeachment, ". . . disgusted everybody." The tenth article of impeachment charged Johnson with bringing "the high office of the President of the United States into contempt, ridicule, and disgrace" by delivering "with a loud voice certain intemperate, inflammatory, and scandalous harangues . . . peculiarly indecent and unbecoming in the Chief Magistrate of the United States."

Though presidential candidates Horatio Seymour in 1868, Rutherford B. Hayes in 1876, and James A. Garfield in 1880 made occasional speeches, only Horace Greeley in 1872, James G. Blaine in 1884, and most spectacularly, William Jennings Bryan in 1896 followed Douglas's audacious example of stumping the country. Such tactics continued to provoke disapproval. Bryan, said John Hay, who had been Lincoln's private secretary and was soon to become McKinley's secretary of state, "is begging for the presidency as a tramp might beg for a pie."

Respectable opinion still preferred the "front porch" campaign, employed by Garfield, by Benjamin Harrison in 1888, and most notably by McKinley in 1896. Here candidates received and addressed numerous delegations at their own homes—a form, as the historian Gil Troy writes, of "stumping in place."

While candidates generally continued to stand on their dignity, popular campaigning in presidential elections flourished in these years, attaining new heights of participation (82 percent of eligible voters in 1876 and never once from 1860 to 1900 under 70 percent) and new wonders of pyrotechnics and ballyhoo. Parties mobilized the electorate as never before, and political iconography was never more ingenious and fantastic. "Politics, considered not as the science of government, but as the art of winning elections and securing office," wrote the keen British observer James Bryce, "has reached in the United States a development surpassing in elaborateness that of England or France as much as the methods of those countries surpass the methods of

Servia or Roumania." Bryce marveled at the "military discipline" of the parties, at "the demonstrations, the parades and receptions, the badges and brass bands and triumphal arches," at the excitement stirred by elections— and at "the disproportion that strikes a European between the merits of the presidential candidate and the blazing enthusiasm which he evokes."

Still the old taboo held back the presidential candidates themselves. Even so irrepressible a campaigner as President Theodore Roosevelt felt obliged to hold his tongue when he ran for reelection in 1904. This unwonted abstinence reminded him, he wrote in considerable frustration, of the July day in 1898 when he was "lying still under shell fire" during the Spanish-American War. "I have continually wished that I could be on the stump myself."

No such constraint inhibited TR, however, when he ran again for the presidency in 1912. Meanwhile, and for the first time, *both* candidates in 1908—Bryan again, and William Howard Taft—actively campaigned for the prize. The duties of the office, on top of the new requirements of campaigning, led Woodrow Wilson to reflect that same year, four years before he himself ran for President, "Men of ordinary physique and discretion cannot be Presidents and live, if the strain be not somehow relieved. We shall be obliged always to be picking our chief magistrates from among wise and prudent athletes,—a small class."

Theodore Roosevelt and Woodrow Wilson combined to legitimate a new conception of presidential candidates as active molders of public opinion in active pursuit of the highest office. Once in the White House, Wilson revived the custom, abandoned by Jefferson, of delivering annual state of the union addresses to Congress in person. In 1916 he became the first incumbent President to stump for his own reelection.

The activist candidate and the bully-pulpit presidency were expressions of the growing democratization of politics. New forms of communication were reconfiguring presidential campaigns. In the nineteenth century the press, far more fiercely partisan then than today, had been the main carrier of political information. In the twentieth century the spread of advertising techniques and the rise of the electronic media—radio, television, computerized public opinion polling—wrought drastic changes in the methodology of politics. In particular the electronic age diminished and now threatens to dissolve the historic role of the party.

The old system had three tiers: the politician at one end; the voter at the other; and the party in between. The party's function was to negotiate between the politician and the voters, interpreting each to the other and providing the link that held the political process together. The electric revolution has substantially abolished the sovereignty of the party. Where once the voter turned to the local party leader to find out whom to support, now he looks at television and makes up his own mind. Where once the politician turned to the local party leader to find out what people are thinking, he now takes a computerized poll.

The electronic era has created a new breed of professional consultants, "handlers," who by the 1980s had taken control of campaigns away from the politicians. The traditional pageantry—rallies, torchlight processions, volunteers, leaflets, billboards, bumper stickers—is now largely a thing of the past. Television replaces the party as the means of mobilizing the voter. And as the party is left to wither on the vine, the presidential candidate becomes more pivotal than ever. We shall see the rise of personalist movements, founded not on historic organizations but on compelling personalities, private fortunes, and popular frustrations. Without the stabilizing influence of parties, American politics would grow angrier, wilder, and more irresponsible.

Things have changed considerably from the austerities of the old republic. Where once voters preferred to call presumably reluctant candidates to the duties of the supreme magistracy and rejected pursuit of the office as evidence of dangerous ambition, now they expect candidates to come to them, explain their views and plead for their support. Where nonpartisan virtue had been the essence, now candidates must prove to voters that they have the requisite "fire in the belly." "'Twud be inth'restin," said Mr. Dooley, ". . . if th' fathers iv th' counthry cud come back an' see what has happened while they've been away. In times past whin ye voted f'r prisident ye didn't vote f'r a man. Ye voted f'r a kind iv a statue that ye'd put up in ye'er own mind on a marble pidistal. Ye nivir heerd iv George Wash'nton goin' around th' counthry distributin' five cint see-gars."

We have reversed the original notion that ambition must be disguised and the office seek the man. Now the man—and soon, one must hope, the woman—seeks the office and does so without guilt or shame or inhibition. This is not necessarily a degradation of democracy. Dropping the disguise is a gain for candor, and personal avowals of convictions and policies may elevate and educate the electorate.

On the other hand, the electronic era has dismally reduced both the intellectual content of campaigns and the attention span of audiences. In the nineteenth century political speeches lasted for a couple of hours and dealt with issues in systematic and exhaustive fashion. Voters drove wagons for miles to hear Webster and Clay, Bryan and Teddy Roosevelt, and felt cheated if the famous orator did not give them their money's worth. Then radio came along and cut political addresses down first to an hour, soon to thirty minutes—still enough time to develop substantive arguments.

But television has shrunk the political talk first to fifteen minutes, now to the sound bite and the thirty-second spot. Advertising agencies today sell candidates with all the cynical contrivance they previously devoted to selling detergents and mouthwash. The result is the debasement of American politics. "The idea that you can merchandise candidates for high office like breakfast cereal," Adlai Stevenson said in 1952, "is the ultimate indignity to the democratic process."

Still Bryce's "intermittent fever" will be upon us every fourth year. We will continue to watch wise if not always prudent athletes in their sprint for the White House, enjoy the quadrennial spectacle and agonize about the outcome.

"The strife of the election," said Lincoln after his reelection in 1864, "is but human-nature practically applied to the facts. What has occurred in this case, must ever recur in similar cases. Human-nature will not change."

Lincoln, as usual, was right. Despite the transformation in political methods there remains a basic continuity in political emotions. "For a long while before the appointed time has come," Tocqueville wrote more than a century and a half ago, "the election becomes the important and, so to speak, the all-engrossing topic of discussion. Factional ardor is redoubled, and all the artificial passions which the imagination can create in a happy and peaceful land are agitated and brought to light. . . .

"As the election draws near, the activity of intrigue and the agitation of the populace increase; the citizens are divided into hostile camps, each of which assumes the name of its favorite candidate; the whole nation glows with feverish excitement; the election is the daily theme of the press, the subject of every private conversation, the end of every thought and every action, the sole interest of the present.

"It is true," Tocqueville added, "that as soon as the choice is determined, this ardor is dispelled, calm returns, and the river, which had nearly broken its banks, sinks to its usual level; but who can refrain from astonishment that such a storm should have arisen?"

The election storm in the end blows fresh and clean. With the tragic exception of 1860, the American people have invariably accepted the result and given the victor their hopes and blessings. For all its flaws and follies, democracy abides.

Let us now turn the pages and watch the gaudy parade of American presidential politics pass by in all its careless glory.

The Election of 1896

Donald A. Ritchie is associate historian of the United States Senate and an adjunct faculty member of the Cornell in Washington program. His books include *James M. Landis: Dean of the Regulators* (1980); *Press Gallery: Congress and the Washington Correspondents* (1991); a high school textbook, *History of a Free Nation* (1991); and *American Journalists: Getting the Story* (1998).

Silver and gold dazzled the depression weary voters of 1896. Both the Democratic and Republican candidates promoted currency reform as a solution to the nation's economic crisis, reversing the parties' historic positions. While the incumbent Democratic President Grover Cleveland clung to the gold standard for stability and fairness to creditors, his party rushed to embrace the coinage of silver to stimulate inflation and ease the burden of debtors. On the Republican side, the front-running contender William McKinley preferred to straddle the currency issue by continuing his support of bimetallism, but conceded to the demands of his party's gold standard advocates. When easterners hammered a strong gold standard plank into the Republican platform, western silverites marched out of the convention in protest. Above in the press box, a tall, young former congressman, now reporting for the Omaha *World-Herald*, climbed upon a desk for a better view of their departure. None of the Republican delegates could have suspected that within three weeks this "interested spectator," William Jennings Bryan, would become the Democratic presidential candidate, under the banner of free silver.

For parades, passions, and the percentage of eligible voters that it attracted to the polls, the campaign of 1896 outdid all others. Its opposing candidates stood in sharp contrast. McKinley was a son of Ohio, the "mother of presidents," and at fifty-three a conventionally conservative politician. A generation younger at thirty-six, Bryan represented the frontier state of Nebraska and dynamic new forces in politics. McKinley, however, had the additional asset of a brilliant campaign manager, Marcus Alonzo Hanna. A coal and iron industrialist from Cleveland, Hanna had raised funds and campaigned for local Republican candidates for decades without earning much notice within his party—until he determined to make McKinley President.

Metal pins with gold and silver coin motifs. The presidential election of 1896 revived political life in America. Free silver became the great rallying cry—the free and unlimited coinage of silver at the ratio to gold of sixteen to one. Resumption by the government of silver coinage would have increased the circulation of paper currency. The resulting inflation, so believed the farmers, would end every agricultural inequity. Free silver became the all-encompassing panacea.

Civil War veteran William McKinley chaired the powerful House Ways and Means Committee and gave his name to the Protective Tariff of 1890. Blaming the McKinley tariff for higher prices, voters that year swept the Republicans out of their congressional majorities and McKinley out of his House seat. Then the economic depression of 1893 shifted voter anger onto the Democrats, resurrecting the status of both the tariff and its namesake. McKinley was a pragmatic politician, highly skilled in the arts of accommodation. One newspaper reporter observed that McKinley's pronounced eyebrows gave his photographs a sternness that this "gentle, kindly disposed man" lacked. Gregarious but "no glad-hander," he had a calm demeanor and subdued sense of humor, attributes that helped him defeat his rival for the nomination, the powerful Speaker of the House Thomas B. Reed, whose wit and biting sarcasm made people uncomfortable, even as they laughed.

With eastern gold standard Republicans favoring Speaker Reed, and "favorite son" candidates holding other delegate blocs, Hanna looked to the southern delegations as the key to the nomination. During the winter of 1895, Hanna rented a house in Georgia, where he and his candidate wooed southern Republicans with promises of future federal patronage. Having secured a majority on the Republican National Committee, which would decide contested seats at the convention, Hanna advised southern party leaders to act as arbitrarily as necessary to elect McKinley delegates. When their opponents bolted and formed separate delegations, the National Committee by wide margins rejected the "bolters" in favor of McKinley's "regulars." This southern strategy netted almost two hundred delegates, a third of McKinley's total, and caused Speaker Reed's unnerved campaign manager to admit to the press that McKinley would be nominated on the first ballot—as he was.

THE LOCKOUT IS ENDED; HE HOLDS THE KEY.

McKinley poster stressing the 1896 economic themes. The gold key will unlock prosperity.

After the convention, Hanna planned a vacation cruise before he returned to run an educational, business-like campaign as chairman of the Republican National Committee. McKinley and Hanna anticipated that their Democratic opponent would be Richard Bland, author of the Bland-Allison Act for limited coinage of silver, and a man as bland as his name. This scenario evaporated when William Jennings Bryan rose to speak in favor of a free silver plank at the Democratic convention. Silver was "a cause as holy as the cause of liberty—the cause of humanity," Bryan declared in a magnificent baritone voice that filled the convention hall without amplification. He called for another Andrew Jackson to speak for the "common people" against organized wealth. Employing the rhetoric of the populist farm movement, he warned urban America: "destroy our farms and the grass will grow in the streets of every city in the country." And he concluded by hurling a powerful metaphor against the opponents of silver: "You shall not press down upon the brow of labor this crown of thorns—you shall not crucify mankind upon a cross of gold."

Bryan stood before the convention with his head hung down and arms outstretched in the image of a crucifixion. For a moment the huge hall remained silent, then "bedlam broke loose, delirium reigned supreme." The

Campaign button with paraphrase of the concluding sentence in Bryan's speech of July 8, 1896, "The Cross of Gold."

Paper hat issued by a Boston newspaper.
Folded another way, it displays
McKinley.

*Washington
Post*'s correspondent
described the yells as "so deafen-
ing that only at irregular intervals could the
music of the noisy band be heard, the stamping of the
feet was as the roll of thunder." The next day, on the fifth ballot, the
Democratic presidential nomination went to Bryan.

Bryan's triumphs disrupted all the other parties. Taken by surprise,
Hanna canceled his vacation plans to revamp Republican strategy. The
Prohibitionist Party split over free silver, and the Populist Party fell
reluctantly into ranks behind Bryan. Populist delegates hated to tie their
party to Bryan's kite, but the professional politicians among them steered
the convention toward fusion. In a futile gesture to preserve what was left
of their separate identity, the Populists nominated their own vice
presidential candidate, Tom Watson of Georgia. The breakaway silver
Republicans nominated Bryan; while gold-standard Cleveland Democrats
formed a national Democratic Party and ran their own candidate.

Few prominent Democrats would campaign for Bryan, nor did many

Mechanical badges which open to reveal the candidates' portraits. Note that McKinley items are gold and the Bryan items are silver.

large newspapers endorse him. Such traditionally Democratic papers as the *New York World*, *Boston Globe*, and *Louisville Courier-Journal* sided with the financial markets against the Democratic candidate. One notable exception was the *New York Journal*, whose publisher, William Randolph Hearst, opposed free silver but endorsed Bryan as a man of the people. Hearst's editorial cartoonist, Homer Davenport, gave the campaign the unforgettable image of "Dollar Mark Hanna," dressed in a checkered suit covered with dollar signs, manipulating a pygmy McKinley. The Dollar Mark cartoons propelled Davenport to fame, diminished McKinley's public image, and wounded Hanna's feelings. Mrs. Hanna hated Davenport "worse than snakes."

Lacking an outlet in the major metropolitan press, and without funds to carry on extensive advertising, an undaunted Bryan took his campaign to the people through a vigorous speaking schedule across the nation. Reporters described Bryan's rear platform oratorical style as "intimate, easy, and colloquial." He spoke in short sentences, using plain words of few syllables. He made his points briefly and drove them home effectively. Biblical quotations and parables scattered throughout his remarks always brought cheers from his audiences. The tremendous crowds convinced Bryan he was going to win.

Bryan's success on the stump made Mark Hanna talk fretfully of sending McKinley out as well, but his candidate rejected the idea. "I might just as well put up a trampoline on my front lawn and compete with some professional athlete as go out speaking against Bryan," McKinley protested. "I have to *think* when I speak." He preferred to read his speeches and even edited the remarks of the leaders of visiting delegations, to avoid indiscreet or divisive references. While he lacked Bryan's dynamism, McKinley possessed a "mesmeric quality" that captured audiences. As celebrated an orator as Wisconsin's Robert La Follette, Sr., rated McKinley "a magnetic speaker" with a "clear, bell-like voice."

McKinley opened his official campaign exactly where he would remain until election day, on his bunting-covered front porch in Canton, Ohio. From that fixed point, McKinley awaited the hundreds of delegations that traveled to Canton by train (at

Walking sticks with Bryan and McKinley metal handles.

Republican ribbon badge from McKinley's hometown, Canton, Ohio. The picture is of Mrs. Ida McKinley.

inexpensive excursion rates), and paraded to his home, all carefully scheduled. The candidate delivered set speeches interspersed with personal references to each of the delegations of farmers, laborers, merchants, and church members that crowded onto his lawn. They totaled an estimated 750,000—more than a tenth of all McKinley voters in the election.

McKinley felt more comfortable talking about tariffs than currency, where his position was less than clear. In Congress, he had voted with bimetallists to override Rutherford B. Hayes's veto of the Bland-Allison bill. While he accepted a gold plank in the platform, he balanced it with a pledge to seek an international agreement on silver, highly unlikely as that was. Friendly reporters counseled McKinley that Bryan had made free silver "practically the only issue of the campaign," and urged him to declare unequivocally against silver. At the end of July, while addressing a Pennsylvania delegation, McKinley proclaimed: "Our currency today is good—all of it as good as gold—and it is the unfaltering determination of the Republican Party to so keep and maintain it forever." Republicans drew a collective sigh of relief, for their candidate at last had said "gold."

Although bowing to gold, McKinley tied it to the themes of protection, prosperity, and

Gold mechanical Republican Party badges that open to show portraits of William McKinley and his vice president, Garret A. Hobart. When Hobart died in office before the 1900 election, he was replaced on the ticket by Theodore Roosevelt.

patriotism. "I am glad to know that this year is going to be a year of patriotism and devotion to country," McKinley told visiting delegations; "that the people of the country this year mean to maintain the financial honor of the country as sacredly as they maintain the honor of the flag."

Delegates wore gold bug lapel pins, and women carried red, white, and blue umbrellas. Hanna also called for all Americans to participate in a national "Flag Day" just before the election, causing Illinois's radical Governor John Peter Altgeld to denounce the McKinley campaign for having "prostituted the American flag to the level of an advertising medium."

Since the Northeast stood solidly Republican, and the South and West were Bryan's territory, both parties looked to the Midwest. Hanna opened an office in Chicago to coordinate publicity and speakers. While McKinley stayed in Canton, the Republican speakers bureau paid 1,400 speakers to stump the nation, and to follow Bryan's campaign train from stop to stop. Republican publicity agents distributed some 200 million pamphlets, many in German, Swedish, French, Spanish, Italian, Norwegian, Finnish, Dutch, and Hebrew.

Silk ribbon with Republican slogans.

Brass stickpin. The Republican Party, both in 1896 and 1900, appealed to laborers with the "Full Dinner Pail" slogan. Reference is to benefits derived from the protective tariff.

Speeches, booklets, posters, and slogans poured out of the Republican headquarters, boosting McKinley as "The Advance Agent of Prosperity" and promising "A Full Dinner Pail" after his election.

Mark Hanna had paid for McKinley's preconvention expenses, $100,000 out of pocket, and took personal charge of raising funds for the campaign. Contributions came from Democratic as well as Republicans bankers and businessmen, appalled by Bryan's free silver platform and rabble-rousing campaign. Reports surfaced throughout the campaign that employers were threatening to reduce wages or cut jobs if Bryan won. To counter charges of intimidation, Republicans organized enormous working-class parades under McKinley's banner. The overwhelming labor vote for McKinley suggested that workers saw his victory in their self interest. As Senator Henry Teller, leader of the silver Republicans, regretfully concluded, "If I were a working man and had nothing but my job, I am afraid when I came to vote I would think of Mollie and the babies."

Bryan's single theme of free silver offered little to labor, but it was the only issue that held together disparate followers from three parties, and inflamed their passions. Occasionally he addressed other issues in the Democratic platform, notably his opposition to federal intervention in labor strikes. The danger came not from small lawbreakers, he asserted, but from "men who think that they are greater than the Government." He promised to enforce antitrust laws and to appoint Supreme Court justices opposed to trusts. Bryan also took pains to explain why some of his agrar-

Mechanical campaign card predicting republican prosperity as opposed to Democratic economic ruin.

ian supporters blamed their economic woes on international Jewish bankers. By denouncing the Rothschilds, he assured Jewish Democrats: "We are not attacking a race; we are attacking greed and avarice, which know neither race nor religion."

Mark Hanna's counterpart, Democratic National Committee chairman James K. Jones, also set up offices in Chicago. But Jones lacked Hanna's tactical genius and cooperative candidate. Bryan, he later reminisced, "was a law unto himself." Senator Jones needed to rebuild the Democratic committee after the departure of the gold Democrats and their campaign contributions. Tight finances especially restricted the production of campaign literature. Bryan's organizational support stemmed less from the party apparatus then from a network of free silver clubs, particularly in rural districts. Since Bryan was running on the Democratic, Populist, and Silver Republican tickets, the clubs attracted a multi-partisan membership. Club members paraded enthusiastically and provided eager audiences for free silver speakers. The clubs also raised money by selling free silver pamphlets, notably William Hope Harvey's *Coin's Financial School*, an immensely popular booklet featuring a young savant who lectured leading financiers on the wisdom of bimetallism.

The 16:1 ratio of silver to gold provided Bryan's supporters the symbolism for their pageantry. At one stop the candidate rode in a carriage drawn by sixteen white horses and one yellow horse. At others he would be greeted by sixteen young women dressed in white, and one in yellow, or presented with similar mixes in chrysanthemums. Well-wishers pressed on Bryan lucky coins, gold-headed canes, a silver watch, and an inkstand shaped like a stack of sixteen silver dollars, with a gold coin as its lid handle.

Traveling in a most inappropriately named railroad car, the "Idler," Bryan conducted a pun-

Political campaign books. This type of book was hastily written and padded with speeches and campaign proceedings

Bryan celluloid buttons. The currency issue dominated the campaign and is so reflected in the artifacts.

ishing campaign. On a single day in Michigan, he spoke—without benefit of the public address systems of a later age—in Muskegon, Holland, Fennville, Bangor, Hartford, Watervliet, Benton Harbor, Niles, Dowagiac, Decatur, Lawrence, Kalamazoo, Battle Creek, Marshall, Albion, Jackson, Leslie, Mason, and Lansing, delivering a total of twenty-five speeches, and finishing near midnight. Desperately afraid of losing his voice, he employed various remedies to soothe his throat after speaking, and catnapped whenever possible between stops. Bryan ended his national tour on election day in Lincoln, Nebraska, where the "Bryan Home Guards" escorted him to vote. For one hundred days he had traveled sixteen thousand miles and given six hundred speeches to an estimated five million listeners. Yet these prodigious personal efforts could not overcome the machine that McKinley and Hanna had constructed.

Although Bryan concentrated on the Midwest, he did not carry such critical states as Wisconsin, Illinois, and Indiana, which Cleveland had won four years earlier. The *New York World* offered a plausible explanation for his failure in the midwestern farm states, noting that the price of wheat had risen from sixty-four to eighty-two cents a bushel the month before the

Porcelain campaign lapel studs.

election. Midwestern wheat farmers could see the end of the depression—which they blamed less on eastern industrialists than on farmers farther west who were flooding the markets and depressing prices.

Nevertheless, currency and economics remained the dominant issues of the campaign. When the *Chicago Record* polled voters it found similar breakdowns in both parties. In their sample, 41 percent of Bryan's voters cited free silver as the most important issue, while 40 percent of McKinley's supporters listed sound money. Smaller percentages of Bryanites cited the income tax, the restoration of prosperity, and opposition to the government's antilabor policies. Only one percent supported Bryan out of traditional Democratic loyalties. Among other Republicans the protective tariff, the needs of farmers and workers, a demand to suppress disorders in the states, and a dislike of Bryan's class-oriented campaigning spurred voters. Only 2 percent said they voted for McKinley because they always leaned Republican.

William Allen White, the Kansas editor, believed that the election had divided the nation between creditors and debtors. "McKinley won because the Republicans had persuaded the middle class, almost to a man, that a threat to the gold standard was a threat to their property." If McKinley appealed to the middle class, Bryan failed to attract the labor vote on his appeal of haves versus have-nots. Labor feared that Bryan's election would shut down the factories, and the Democrats could not overcome their image as the party of the "empty dinner pail." Even farmers, Bryan's core constituency, divided between the needier westerners and more prosperous midwesterners. Moreover, Bryan's rural America was dwindling; only two decades later the census would show a majority of the population living in urban areas.

The election marked the end of one political era and the beginning of another. After a generation of partisan stalemate, the Republicans now claimed a solid electoral majority. The currency issue became irrelevant when new discoveries of gold in South Africa and the

Gold-painted metal mantle clock with shipping and industry themes.

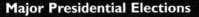

McKinley campaign umbrella.

Yukon brought about through gold the inflated currency that the silver movement had promised. New demands for agricultural products from Europe and America's growing cities stimulated a generation of farm prosperity. The middle and upper classes, frightened by Bryan and the Populists, began to move toward a new progressive reform movement that expropriated and enacted into law much of Bryan's platform. At the same time, partisan display diminished. After 1896, marching clubs and torchlight parades became less common, along with the use of floats, banners, glee clubs, brass bands, all-day rallies, and other nineteenth century devices to stimulate voter enthusiasm.

When the cheering stopped, McKinley went to the White House to become a beloved and martyred President. Bryan, in losing his election, won a higher total and a higher percentage of the votes cast in 1896 than would elect Woodrow Wilson in 1912. He lost two more campaigns for the presidency and spent the rest of his life as a troubadour in search of a crowd and an issue as congenial as free silver. Still, his first battle won widespread admiration even from such unlikely sources as Nannie Lodge, wife of Senator Henry Cabot Lodge, the author of the Republican gold standard plank. "The great fight is won," she wrote to a British friend after the election:

> . . . a fight conducted by trained and experienced and organized forces, with both hands full of money, with the power of the press—and of prestige—on one side: on the other, a disorganized mob at first, out of which burst into sight, hearing, and force—one man, but such a man! Alone, penniless, without backing, without money, with scarce a paper, without speakers, that man fought such a fight that even those in the East can call him a Crusader, an inspired fanatic—a prophet! It has been marvelous. . . . We had during the last week of the campaign 18,000 speakers on the stump. He alone spoke for his party, but speeches which spoke to the intelligence and parts of the people, and with a capital P. It is over now, but the vote is 7 millions to 6 millions and a half.

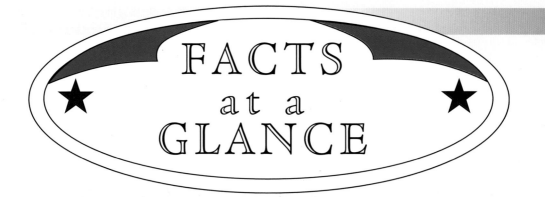

FACTS at a GLANCE

WILLIAM MCKINLEY

- **Born:** January 29, 1843, in Niles, Ohio
- **Parents:** William and Nancy Campbell Allison McKinley
- **Education:** attended Allegheny College (Pennsylvania) and Albany (New York) Law School
- **Occupation:** Lawyer, politician
- **Married:** Ida Saxton (1847–1907) on January 25, 1871
- **Children:** Katherine McKinley (1871–75); Ida McKinley (1873)
- **Died:** September 14, 1901, at Buffalo, New York

Served as the 25TH PRESIDENT OF THE UNITED STATES,

- March 4, 1897, to September 14, 1901

VICE PRESIDENTS

- Garret A. Hobart (1897–99)
- Theodore Roosevelt (1901)

Satirical mechanical "broken dollar" comparing the prosperity of sound money with the economic ruin of free silver. Front and back views.

CABINET

Secretary of State
- John Sherman (1897–98)
- William R. Day (1898)
- John M. Hay (1898–1901)

Secretary of the Treasury
- Lyman J. Gage (1897–1901)

Secretary of War
- Russel A. Alger (1897–99)
- Elihu Root (1899–1901)

Attorney General
- Joseph McKenna (1897–98)
- John W. Griggs (1898-1901)
- Philander C. Knox (1901)

Postmaster General
- James A. Gary (1897–98)
- Charles Emory Smith (1898–1901)

Secretary of the Navy
- John D. Long (1897–1901)

Secretary of the Interior
- Cornelius N. Bliss (1897–99)
- Ethan A. Hitchcock (1899–1901)

Secretary of Agriculture
- James Wilson (1897–1901)

OTHER POLITICAL POSITIONS

- Member of the U.S. House of Representatives, 1877–91

- Governor of Ohio, 1892–96

NOTABLE EVENTS DURING MCKINLEY'S ADMINISTRATION

1897   William McKinley is sworn in as the 25th president of the United States on March 4; the Dingley Tariff, which increases rates on imported goods, is signed into law.

1898   In February the battleship *Maine* explodes in Havana harbor, increasing anti-Spanish sentiment in the United States; on April 25, the U.S. declares war on Spain; an armistice is agreed to in August.

1899   The senate ratifies the Treaty of Paris, which ends the Spanish-American War; Secretary of State John Hay establishes the "Open Door Policy," which says that all countries should have equal access to China for trade purposes; vice president Garret Hobart dies in office.

1900   U.S. troops are sent to China to rescue Americans stranded in that country by the Boxer Rebellion; the Gold Standard Act becomes law; McKinley is reelected by a wide margin over William Jennings Bryan.

1901   McKinley is inaugurated for the second time on March 4; visits the Pan-American Exposition in Buffalo, New York, in September, where he is shot by anarchist Leon Czolgosz on September 6; dies September 14, and vice president Theodore Roosevelt is sworn in as president.

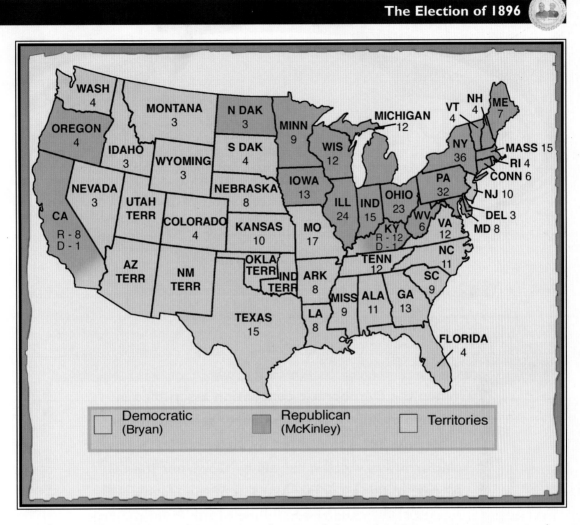

| Democratic (Bryan) | Republican (McKinley) | Territories |

Though William Jennings Bryan carried most of the midwestern states as expected, he could not capture three crucial states that had voted Democratic in 1892—Illinois, Wisconsin, and Indiana. These 51 electoral votes would have swung the election to Bryan. Instead, William McKinley won the industrial north and far west to gain a strong victory over the Democrat. McKinley received 271 electoral votes and 51.1 percent of the popular vote to 176 electoral votes and 47.7 percent of the popular vote for Bryan. Third-party candidates—most notably the National (Gold) Democrats, Prohibitionists, and Socialists—collected just 1.2 percent of the vote nationally.

★ Democratic Party Platform of 1896 ★

When the Democratic convention assembled in Chicago on July 7, 1896, the party seemed not only leaderless but also divided by bitter strife. The party platform was written largely by Governor John P. Altgeld of Illinois whose pardon of the Haymarket rioters (1893) and the handling of the Pullman strike (1894) had made him hated by conservatives everywhere. The platform repudiated many of President Grover Cleveland's policies and came out flatly for *unlimited* coinage of silver at the ratio of sixteen ounces of silver to one ounce of gold, which Cleveland firmly labeled as "dangerous and reckless." But state convention after convention had chosen delegates pledged to the silver crusade. The uncompromising silver platform plank, adopted 628 to 301, indicated that the bimetallists had won a majority of the delegates.

We, the Democrats of the United States in National Convention assembled, do reaffirm our allegiance to those great essential principles of justice and liberty, upon which our institutions are founded, and which the Democratic Party has advocated from Jefferson's time to our own— freedom of speech, freedom of the press, freedom of conscience, the preservation of personal rights, the equality of all citizens before the law, and the faithful observance of constitutional limitations.

During all these years the Democratic Party has resisted the tendency of selfish interests to the centralization of governmental power, and steadfastly maintained the integrity of the dual scheme of government established by the founders of this Republic of republics. Under its guidance and teachings the great principle of local self-government has found its best expression in the maintenance of the rights of the States and in its assertion of the necessity of confining the general government to the exercise of the powers granted by the Constitution of the United States.

The Constitution of the United States guarantees to every citizen the rights of civil and religious liberty. The Democratic Party has always been the exponent of political liberty and religious freedom, and it renews its obligations and reaffirms its devotion to these fundamental principles of the Constitution.

The Money Plank

Recognizing that the money question is paramount to all others at this time, we invite attention to the fact that the Federal Constitution named silver and gold together as the money metals of the United States, and that the first coinage law passed by Congress under the Constitution made the silver dollar the monetary unit and admitted gold to free coinage at a ratio based upon the silver-dollar unit.

We declare that the act of 1873 demonetizing silver without the

Cotton bandanna
with major slogans
of the Democratic
Party.

knowledge or approval of the American people has resulted in the apprecia-
tion of gold and a corresponding fall in the prices of commodities produced by
the people; a heavy increase in the burdens of taxation and of all debts,
public and private; the enrichment of the money-lending class at home and
abroad; the prostration of industry and impoverishment of the people.

We are unalterably opposed to monometallism which has locked fast the
prosperity of an industrial people in the paralysis of hard times. Gold
monometallism is a British policy, and its adoption has brought other nations
into financial servitude to London. It is not only un-American but anti-
American, and it can be fastened on the United States only by the stifling of
that spirit and love of liberty which proclaimed our political independence in
1776 and won it in the War of the Revolution.

We demand the free and unlimited coinage of both silver and gold at the present legal ratio of 16 to 1 without waiting for the aid or consent of any other nation. We demand that the standard silver dollar shall be a full legal tender, equally with gold, for all debts, public and private, and we favor such legislation as will prevent for the future the demonetization of any kind of legal-tender money by private contract.

We are opposed to the policy and practice of surrendering to the holders of the obligations of the United States the option reserved by law to the Government of redeeming such obligations in either silver coin or gold coin. [. . .]

Tariff Resolution

We hold that tariff duties should be levied for purposes of revenue, such duties to be so adjusted as to operate equally throughout the country, and not discriminate between class or section, and that taxation should be limited by the needs of the Government, honestly and economically administered. We denounce as disturbing to business the Republican threat to restore the McKinley law, which has twice been condemned by the people in National elections and which, enacted under the false plea of protection to home industry, proved a prolific breeder of trusts and monopolies, enriched the few at the expense of the many, restricted trade and deprived the producers of the great American staples of access to their natural markets.

Until the money question is settled we are opposed to agitation for further changes in our tariff laws, except such as are necessary to meet the deficit in revenue caused by the adverse decision of the Supreme Court on the income tax. But for this decision by the Supreme Court, there would be no deficit in the revenue under the law passed by the Democratic Congress in strict pursuance of the uniform decisions of that court for nearly 100 years, that court having in that decision sustained Constitutional objections to its enactment which had previously been over-ruled by the ablest Judges who have ever sat on that bench. We declare that it is the duty of Congress to use all the

Constitutional power which remains after that decision, or which may come from its reversal by the court as it may after be constituted, so that the burdens of taxation may be equally and impartially laid, to the end that wealth may bear its due proportion of the expense of the Government.

Immigration and Arbitration

We hold that the most efficient way of protecting American labor is to prevent the importation of foreign pauper labor to compete with it in the home market, and that the value of the home market to our American farmers and artisans is greatly reduced by a vicious monetary system which depresses the prices of our products below the cost of production, and thus deprives them of the means of purchasing the products of our home manufactories; and as labor creates the wealth of the country, we demand the passage of such laws as may be necessary to protect it in all its rights.

We are in favor of the arbitration of differences between employers engaged in interstate commerce and their employees, and recommend such legislation as is necessary to carry out this principle.

Trusts and Pools

The absorption of wealth by the few, the consolidation of our leading railroad systems, and the formation of trusts and pools require a stricter control by the Federal Government of those arteries of commerce. We demand the enlargement of the powers of the Interstate Commerce Commission and such restriction and guarantees in the control of railroads as will protect the people from robbery and oppression. [. . .]

Federal Interference in Local Affairs

We denounce arbitrary interference by Federal authorities in local affairs as a violation of the Constitution of the United States, and a crime against free institutions, and we especially object to government by injunction as a

Cotton bandanna with slogan "the poor man's candidates."

new and highly dangerous form of oppression by which Federal Judges, in contempt of the laws of the States and rights of citizens, become at once legislators, judges and executioners; and we approve the bill passed at the last session of the United States Senate, and now pending in the House of Representatives, relative to contempts in Federal courts and providing for trials by jury in certain cases of contempt.

Pacific Railroad

No discrimination should be indulged in by the Government of the United States in favor of any of its debtors. We approve of the refusal of the Fifty-Third Congress to pass the Pacific Railroad Funding bill and denounce the effort of the present Republican Congress to enact a similar measure.

Pensions

Recognizing the just claims of deserving Union soldiers, we heartily indorse the rule of the present Commissioner of Pensions, that no names shall be arbitrarily dropped from the pension roll; and that the fact of enlistment and service should be deemed conclusive evidence against disease and disability before enlistment.

Admission of Territories

We favor the admission of the Territories of New Mexico, Arizona and Oklahoma into the Union as States, and we favor the early admission of all the Territories, having the necessary population and resources to entitle them to Statehood, and, while they remain Territories, we hold that the officials appointed to administer the government of any Territory, together with the District of Columbia and Alaska, should be bona-fide residents of the Territory or District in which their duties are to be performed. The Democratic Party believes in home rule and that all public lands of the United States should be appropriated to the establishment of free homes for American citizens.

We recommend that the Territory of Alaska be granted a delegate in Congress and that the general land and timber laws of the United States be extended to said Territory.

Sympathy for Cuba

The Monroe doctrine, as originally declared, and as interpreted by succeeding Presidents, is a permanent part of the foreign policy of the United States, and must at all times be maintained.

We extend our sympathy to the people of Cuba in their heroic struggle for liberty and independence.

Civil-Service Laws

We are opposed to life tenure in the public service, except as provided in the Constitution. We favor appointments based on merit, fixed terms of office, and such an administration of the civil-service laws as will afford equal opportunities to all citizens of ascertained fitness.

Third-Term Resolution

We declare it to be the unwritten law of this Republic, established by custom and usage of 100 years, and sanctioned by the examples of the greatest and wisest of those who founded and have maintained our Government that no man should be eligible for a third term of the Presidential office.

Improvement of Waterways

The Federal Government should care for and improve the Mississippi River and other great waterways of the Republic, so as to secure for the interior States easy and cheap transportation to tidewater. When any water-way of the Republic is of sufficient importance to demand aid of the Government such aid should be extended upon a definite plan of continuous work until permanent improvement is secured.

Conclusion

Confiding in the justice of our cause and the necessity of its success at the polls, we submit the foregoing declaration of principles and purposes to the considerate judgment of the American people. We invite the support of all citizens who approve them and who desire to have them made effective through legislation, for the relief of the people and the restoration of the country's prosperity.

★ Republican Party ★ Platform of 1896

The 1896 Republican national convention showed its solidarity by nominating on the first ballot William McKinley of Ohio, sponsor of the high protective tariff of 1890. McKinley was handpicked by his fellow Ohioan Mark Hanna, the shipping magnate who was emerging as the Republican national boss.

Hanna wanted McKinley to straddle the money issue to keep silverite Republicans from leaving the party. But, he yielded to a sound-money plank endorsing the gold standard in return for eastern corporate financial support in the campaign. Although as a congressman, McKinley had backed prosilver bills, he now assured eastern Republicans of his complete acceptance of the gold plank. Thirty-four western delegates pledged to free silver, led by Senator Henry Teller of Colorado, bolted the convention and urged their followers to support Bryan. The issue between the parties was clearly drawn.

The Republicans of the United States, assembled by their representatives in National Convention, appealing for the popular and historical justification of their claims to the matchless achievements of thirty years of Republican rule, earnestly and confidently address themselves to the awakened intelligence, experience and conscience of their countrymen in the following declaration of facts and principles:

For the first time since the civil war the American people have witnessed the calamitous consequence of full and unrestricted Democratic control of the government. It has been a record of unparalleled incapacity, dishonor and disaster. In administrative management it has ruthlessly sacrificed indispensable revenue, entailed an unceasing deficit, eked out ordinary current expenses with borrowed money, piled up the public debt by $262,000,000 in time of peace, forced an adverse balance of trade, kept a perpetual menace hanging over the redemption fund, pawned American credit to alien syndicates and reversed all the measures and results of successful Republican rule. In the broad effect of its policy it has precipitated panic, blighted industry and trade with prolonged depression, closed factories, reduced work and wages, halted enterprise and crippled American production, while stimulating foreign production for the American market. Every consideration of public safety and individual interest demands that the government shall be wrested from the hands of those who have shown themselves incapable of conducting it without disaster at home and dishonor abroad and shall be restored to the party which for thirty years administered it with unequaled success and prosperity. And in this connection, we heartily endorse the wisdom, patriotism and success of the administration of Benjamin Harrison. We renew and emphasize our allegiance to the policy of protection, as the bulwark of American industrial independence, and the foundation of American development and prosperity. This true American policy taxes foreign products and encourages home industry. It puts the burden of revenue on foreign goods; it secures the American market for the American producer. It upholds the American standard of wages for the American workingman; it puts the factory by the side of the farm and makes the American farmer less dependent on foreign demand and price; it diffuses general thrift, and founds the strength of all on the strength of each. In its reasonable application it is just, fair and impartial, equally opposed to foreign control and domestic monopoly to sectional discrimination and individual favoritism.

We denounce the present tariff as sectional, injurious to the public credit and destructive to business enterprise. We demand such an equitable tariff on foreign imports which come into competition with the American products as will not only furnish adequate revenue for the necessary expenses of the Government, but will protect American labor from degradation and the wage level of other lands. We are not pledged to any particular schedules. The question of rates is a practical question, to be governed by the conditions of time and of production. The ruling and uncompromising principle is the protection and development of American labor and industries. The country demands a right settlement, and then it wants rest.

We believe the repeal of the reciprocity arrangements negotiated by the last Republican Administration was a National calamity, and demand their renewal and extension on such terms as will equalize our trade with other nations, remove the restrictions which now obstruct the sale of American products in the ports of other countries, and secure enlarged markets for the products of our farms, forests, and factories.

Protection and Reciprocity are twin measures of American policy and go hand in hand. Democratic rule has recklessly struck down both, and both must be re-established. Protection for what we produce; free admission for the necessaries of life which we do not produce; reciprocal arrangement of mutual interests, which gain open markets for us in return for our open markets for others. Protection builds up domestic industry and trade and secures our own

Cotton bandanna with major slogans of the Republican Party.

market for ourselves; reciprocity builds up foreign trade and finds an outlet for our surplus. We condemn the present administration for not keeping [faith] with the sugar producers of this country. The Republican Party favors such protection as will lead to the production on American soil of all the sugar which the American people use, and for which they pay other countries more than one hundred million dollars annually. To all our products; to those of the mine and the fields, as well as to those of the shop and the factory, to hemp and wool, the product of the great industry sheep husbandry; as well as to the foundry, as to the mills, we promise the most ample protection. We favor the early American policy of discriminating duties for the upbuilding of our merchant marine. To the protection of our shipping in the foreign-carrying trade, so that American ships, the product of American labor, employed in American ship-yards, sailing under the stars and stripes, and manned, officered and owned by Americans, may regain the carrying of our foreign commerce.

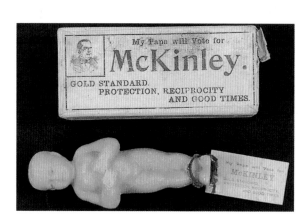

Soap baby proclaiming "My papa will vote for McKinley."

The Republican Party is unreservedly for sound money. It caused the enactment of a law providing for the [resumption] of specie payments in 1879. Since then every dollar has been as good as gold. We are unalterably opposed to every measure calculated to debase our currency or impair the credit of our country. We are therefore opposed to the free coinage of silver, except by international agreement with the leading commercial nations of the earth, which agreement we pledge ourselves to promote, and until such agreement can be obtained the existing gold standard must be maintained. All of our silver and paper currency must be maintained at parity with gold, and we favor all measures designated to maintain inviolable the obligations of the United States, of all our money, whether coin or paper, at the present standard, the standard of most enlightened nations of the earth.

The veterans of the Union Armies deserve and should receive fair treatment and generous recognition. Whenever practicable they should be given the preference in the matter of employment. And they are entitled to the enactment of such laws as are best calculated to secure the fulfillment of the pledges made to them in the dark days of the country's peril.

We denounce the practice in the pension bureau so recklessly and unjustly carried on by the present Administration of reducing pensions and arbitrarily dropping names from the rolls, as deserving the severest condemnation of the American people.

Our foreign policy should be at all times firm, vigorous and dignified, and all our interests in the western hemisphere should be carefully watched and guarded.

The Hawaiian Islands should be controlled by the United States, and no foreign power should be permitted to interfere with them. The Nicaragua Canal should be built, owned and operated by the United States. And, by the purchase of the Danish Islands we should secure a much-needed Naval station in the West Indies.

The massacres in Armenia have aroused the deep sympathy and just indignation of the American people, and we believe that the United States should exercise all the influence it can properly exert to bring these atrocities to an end. In Turkey, American residents have been exposed to [grievous] dangers and American property destroyed. There, and everywhere, American citizens and American property must be absolutely protected at all hazards and at any cost.

We reassert the Monroe Doctrine in its full extent, and we reaffirm the rights of the United States to give the Doctrine effect by responding to the appeal of any American State for friendly intervention in case of European encroachment.

We have not interfered and shall not interfere, with the existing possession of any European power in this hemisphere, and to the ultimate union of all the English speaking parts of the continent by the free consent of its inhabitants; from the hour of achieving their own independence of the people of the United States have regarded with sympathy the struggles of other American peoples to free themselves from European domination. We watch with deep and abiding interest the heroic battles of the Cuban patriots against cruelty and oppression, and best hopes go out for the full success of their determined contest for liberty. The government of Spain, having lost control of Cuba, and being unable to protect the property or lives of resident American citizens, or to comply with its Treaty obligations, we believe that the government of the United States should actively use its influence and good offices to restore peace and give independence to the Island.

The peace and security of the Republic and the maintenance of its rightful influence among the nations of the earth demand a naval power commensurate with its position and responsibilities. We, therefore, favor the continued enlargement of the navy, and a complete system of harbor and sea-coast defenses.

For the protection of the equality of our American citizenship and of the wages of our workingmen, against the fatal competition of low priced labor, we demand that the immigration laws be thoroughly enforced, and so extended as to exclude from entrance to the United States those who can neither read nor write.

The civil service law was placed on the statute book by the Republican Party which has always sustained it, and we renew our repeated declarations that it shall be thoroughly and heartily, and honestly enforced, and extended wherever practicable.

We demand that every citizen of the United States shall be allowed to cast one free and unrestricted ballot, and that such ballot shall be counted and returned as cast.

We proclaim our unqualified condemnation of the uncivilized and preposterous practice well known as lynching, and killing of human beings suspected or charged with crime without process of law.

We favor the creation of a National Board of Arbitration to settle and adjust differences which may arise between employers and employed engaged in inter-State commerce.

We believe in an immediate return to the free homestead policy of the Republican Party, and urge the passage by Congress of a satisfactory free homestead measure which has already passed the House, and is now pending in the senate.

We favor the admission of the remaining Territories at the earliest practicable date having due regard to the interests of the people of the Territories and of the United States. And the Federal officers appointed for the Territories should be selected from the bona-fide residents thereof, and the right to self-government should be accorded them as far as practicable.

We believe that the citizens of Alaska should have representation in the Congress of the United States, to the end that needful legislation may be intelligently enacted.

We sympathize fully with all legitimate efforts to lesson and prevent the evils of intemperance and promote morality. The Republican Party is mindful of the rights and interests of women, and believes that they should be accorded equal opportunities, equal pay for equal work, and protection to the home. We favor the admission of women to wider spheres of usefulness and welcome their co-operation in rescuing the country from Democratic and Populist mismanagement and misrule.

Such are the principles of the Republican Party. By these principles we will apply it to those policies and put them into execution. We rely on the faithful and considerate judgment of the American people, confident alike of the history of our great party and in the justice of our cause, and we present our platform and our candidates in the full assurance that their selection will bring victory to the Republican Party, and prosperity to the people of the United States.

McKinley cane with a gold handle.

The People's [Populist] Party Platform

The Populists decided to hold their national convention after the Republicans and Democrats had met. Their leaders calculated that if both their rivals nominated advocates of the gold standard then the Populists would have the only candidate for free silver.

Bryan's selection upset the Populist strategy and placed the party in a precarious predicament. If they, too, nominated Bryan and fused their campaign with the Democrats, then why should they remain a third party? "If we fuse, we are sunk," said one leader, but "if we don't fuse, all the silver men will leave us for the powerful Democrats." After a rancorous meeting, the Populists nominated Bryan and accepted free silver as the paramount issue. But, they tried to save their separate identity by selecting Thomas E. Watson of Georgia as their vice presidential candidate. With William Jennings Bryan, the forces of agrarian discontent, at long last, had found a spokesman.

The People's Party, assembled in National Convention, reaffirms its allegiance to the principles declared by the founders of the Republic, and also to the fundamental principles of just government as enunciated in the platform of the party in 1892.

We recognize that through the connivance of the present and preceding Administrations the country has reached a crisis in its National life, as predicted in our declaration four years ago, and that prompt and patriotic action is the supreme duty of the hour.

We realize that, while we have political independence, our financial and industrial independence is yet to be attained by restoring to our country the Constitutional control and exercise of the functions necessary to a people's government, which functions have been basely surrendered by our public servants to corporate monopolies. The influence of European moneychangers has been more potent in shaping legislation than the voice of the American people. Executive power and patronage have been used to corrupt our legislatures and defeat the will of the people, and plutocracy has thereby been enthroned upon the ruins of democracy. To restore the Government intended by the fathers, and for the welfare and prosperity of this and future generations, we demand the establishment of an economic and financial system which shall make us masters of our own affairs and independent of European control, by the adoption of the following declaration of principles:

The Finances

We demand a National money, safe and sound, issued by the General Government only, without the intervention of banks of issue, to be a full legal tender for all debts, public and private; a just, equitable, and efficient means of distribution, direct to the people, and through the lawful disbursements of the Government.

We demand the free and unrestricted coinage of silver and gold at the present legal ratio of 16 to 1, without waiting for the consent of foreign nations.

We demand that the volume of circulating medium be speedily increased to an amount sufficient to meet the demand of the business and population, and to restore the just level of prices of labor and production.

We denounce the sale of bonds and the increase of the public interest-bearing debt made by the present Administration as unnecessary and without authority of law, and demand that no more bonds be issued, except by specific act of Congress.

We demand such legislation as will prevent the demonetization of the lawful money of the United States by private contract.

We demand that the Government, in payment of its obligation, shall use its option as to the kind of lawful money in which they are to be paid, and we denounce the present and preceding Administrations for surrendering this option to the holders of Government obligations.

We demand a graduated income tax, to the end that aggregated wealth shall bear its just proportion of taxation, and we regard the recent decision of the Supreme Court relative to the income-tax law as a misinterpretation of the Constitution and an invasion of the rightful powers of Congress over the subject of taxation.

We demand that postal savings-banks be established by the Government for the safe deposit of the savings of the people and to facilitate exchange.

Railroads and Telegraphs

Transportation being a means of exchange and a public necessity, the Government should own and operate the railroads in the interest of the people and on a non-partisan basis, to the end that all may be accorded the same treatment in transportation, and that the tyranny and political power now exercised by the great railroad corporations, which result in the impairment, if not the destruction of the political rights and personal liberties of the citizens, may be destroyed. Such ownership is to be accomplished gradually, in a manner consistent with sound public policy.

The interest of the United States in the public highways built with public moneys, and the proceeds of grants of land to the Pacific railroads, should never be alienated, mortgaged, or sold, but guarded and protected for the general welfare, as provided by the laws organizing such railroads. The foreclosure of existing liens of the United States on these roads should at once follow default in the payment thereof by the debtor companies; and at the foreclosure sales of said roads the Government shall purchase the same, if it becomes necessary to protect its interests therein, or if they can be purchased at a reasonable price; and the Government shall operate said railroads as public highways for the benefit of the whole people, and not in the interest of the few, under suitable provisions for protection of life and property, giving to all transportation interests equal privileges and equal rates for fares and freight.

We denounce the present infamous schemes for refunding these debts, and demand that the laws now applicable thereto be executed and administered according to their intent and spirit.

The telegraph, like the Post Office system, being a necessity for the transmission of news, should be owned and operated by the Government in the interest of the people.

The Public Lands

True policy demands that the National and State legislation shall be such as will ultimately enable every prudent and industrious citizen to secure a home, and therefore the land should not be monopolized for speculative purposes. All lands now held by railroads and other corporations in excess of their actual needs should by lawful means be reclaimed by the Government and held for actual settlers only, and private land monopoly, as well as alien ownership, should be prohibited.

We condemn the land grant frauds by which the Pacific railroad companies have, through the connivance of the Interior Department, robbed multitudes of bona-fide settlers of their homes and miners of their claims, and we demand legislation by Congress which will enforce the exemption of mineral land from such grants after as well as before the patent.

We demand that bona-fide settlers on all public lands be granted free homes, as provided in the National Homestead Law, and that no exception be made in the case of Indian reservations when opened for settlement, and that all lands not now patented come under this demand.

The Referendum

We favor a system of direct legislation through the initiative and referendum, under proper Constitutional safeguards.

Direct Election of President and Senators by the People

We demand the election of President, Vice-President, and United States Senators by a direct vote of the people.

Sympathy for Cuba

We tender to the patriotic people of Cuba our deepest sympathy for their heroic struggle for political freedom and independence, and we believe the time has come when the United States, the great Republic of the world, should recognize that Cuba is, and of right out to be, a free and independent state.

The Territories

We favor home rule in the Territories and the District of Columbia, and the early admission of the Territories as States.

Public Salaries

All public salaries should be made to correspond to the price of labor and its products.

Employment to be Furnished by Government

In times of great industrial depression, idle labor should be employed on public works as far as practicable. [. . .]

A Fair Ballot

Believing that the elective franchise and an untrammeled ballot are essential to a government of, for, and by the people, the People's Party condemns the wholesale system of disfranchisement adopted in some States as unrepublican and undemocratic, and we declare it the duty of the several State legislatures to take such action as will secure a full, free and fair ballot and an honest count.

The Financial Question "The Pressing Issue"

While the foregoing propositions constitute the platform upon which our party stands, and for the vindication of which its organization will be maintained, we recognize that the great and pressing issue of the pending campaign, upon which the present election will turn, is the financial question, and upon this great and specific issue between the parties we cordially invite the aid and co-operation of all organizations and citizens agreeing with us upon this vital question.

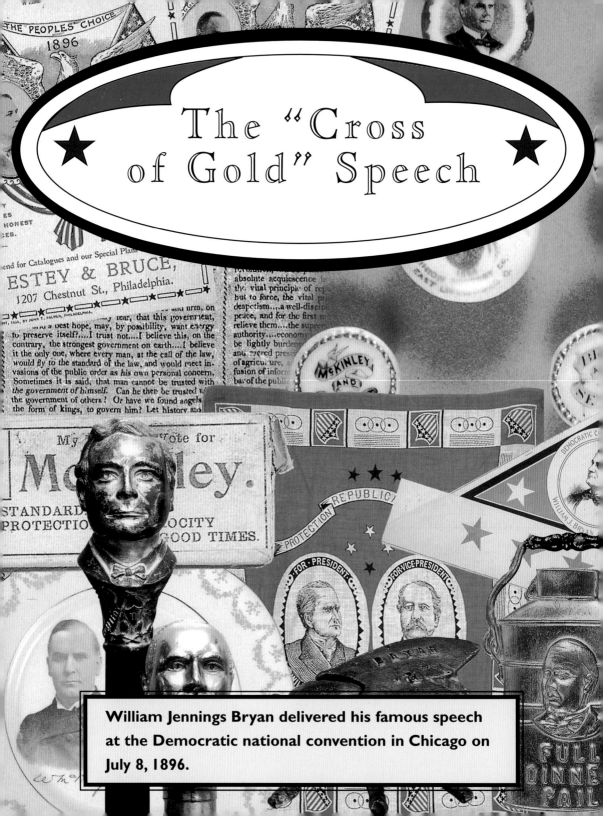

The "Cross of Gold" Speech

William Jennings Bryan delivered his famous speech at the Democratic national convention in Chicago on July 8, 1896.

I would be presumptuous, indeed, to present myself against the distinguished gentlemen to whom you have listened if this were a mere measuring of abilities; but this is not a contest between persons. The humblest citizen in all the land, when clad in the armor of a righteous cause, is stronger than all the hosts of error. I come to speak to you in defense of a cause as holy as the cause of liberty—the cause of humanity.

When this debate is concluded, a motion will be made to lay upon the table the resolution offered in commendation of the administration, and also the resolution offered in condemnation of the administration. We object to bringing this question down to the level of persons. The individual is but an atom; he is born, he acts, he dies; but principles are eternal; and this has been a contest over a principle.

Never before in the history of this country has there been witnessed such a contest as that through which we have just passed. Never before in the history of American politics has a great issue been fought out as this issue has been, by the voters of a great party. On the fourth of March, 1895, a few Democrats, most of them members of Congress, issued an address to the Democrats of the nation, asserting that the money question was the paramount issue of the hour; declaring that a majority of the Democratic Party had the right to control the action of the party on this paramount issue; and concluding with the request that the believers in the free coinage of silver in the Democratic Party should organize, take charge of, and control the policy of the Democratic Party. Three months later, at Memphis, an organization was perfected, and the Silver Democrats went forth openly and courageously proclaiming their belief, and declaring that, if successful, they would crystallize into a platform the declaration which they had made. Then began the conflict. With a zeal approaching the zeal which inspired the crusaders who followed Peter the Hermit, our silver Democrats went forth from victory unto victory until they are now assembled, not to discuss, not to debate, but to enter up the judgment already rendered by the plain people of this country. In this contest brother has been arrayed against brother, father against son. The warmest ties of love, acquaintance and association have been disregarded; old leaders have been cast aside when they have refused to give expression to the sentiments of those whom they would lead, and new leaders have sprung up to give direction to this cause of truth. Thus has the contest been waged, and we have assembled here under as binding and solemn instructions as were ever imposed upon representatives of the people.

We do not come as individuals. As individuals we might have been glad to compliment the gentleman from New York, Senator Hill, but we know that the people for whom we speak would never be willing to put him in a position where he could thwart the will of the Democratic Party. I say it was not a question of persons; it was a question of principle, and it is not with gladness, my friends, that we find ourselves brought into conflict with those who are now arrayed on the other side.

The gentleman who preceded me, ex-Governor Russell, spoke of the State of Massachusetts; let me assure him that not one person in all this convention entertains the least hostility to the people of the State of Massachusetts, but we stand here representing people who are the equals, before the law, of the greatest citizens in the State of Massachusetts. When you come before us and tell us that we are about to disturb your business interests, we reply that you have disturbed our business interests by your course.

We say to you that you have made the definition of a business man too limited in its application. The man who is employed for wages is as much a business man as his employer, the attorney in a country town is as much a business man as the corporation counsel in a great metropolis; the merchant at the crossroads store is as much a business man as the merchant of New York; the farmer who goes forth in the morning and toils all day—who begins in the spring and toils all summer—and who by the application of brain and

To many, the currency issue seems complicated because it is difficult to grasp that from 1792 to 1933, paper money was interchangeable with either gold and/or silver. Since 1933, when the United States went off the gold standard, money is backed by "faith and credit" of the government. Therefore, in theory, there is no limit now to the amount of currency the government can choose to issue. Today we accept paper money without thinking that these notes had once been backed by a precious metal, a centuries-old tradition.

From the ancient world on, gold and silver have been found in nature in almost a set ratio to each other and these two metals were used as monies. However, new silver deposits discovered in the West after the Civil War, especially in Nevada, led to an overabundance of silver and virtually wiped out the traditional ratio of these metals to each other. This caused the price of silver to drop on the open market. An inflation would occur if silver were coined by the government at the same value ratio to gold as had been in effect prior to the discovery of the new silver deposits. A debtor, for example, would be able to repay debts with a "cheaper" dollar—that is, the amount of silver in the coin would be worth less than the monetary value stamped on the coin. Labor groups believed that the resulting inflation would both raise farm prices and industrial wages.

In 1878, the House of Representatives, dominated by inflationists, passed the Bland Bill, sponsored by Richard P. Bland, which provided for the unlimited coinage of silver at the ratio of 16 to 1, a coinage ratio in effect prior to the discovery of vast new silver deposits. Weakened by a Senate amendment introduced by William Allison, the bill finally passed over President Hayes's veto. Bland-Allison provided for the purchase of silver from mines by the government but not the coinage of the metal. Therefore the effect of the act was not inflationary. Instead, the purchase of silver was a government subsidy to silver mine owners.

The money issue became an emotional one in the decades after the Civil War as millions believed that their economic well-being was determined by monetary policy. This dispute over the issue of gold and silver as the backing for currency would reach its zenith during the 1896 presidential election.

muscle to the natural resources of the country creates wealth, is as much a business man as the man who goes upon the board of trade and bets upon the price of grain; the miners who go down a thousand feet into the earth, or climb two thousand feet upon the cliffs, and bring forth from their hiding places the precious metals to be poured into the channels of trade are as much business men as the few financial magnates who, in a back room, corner the money of the world. We come to speak for this broader class of business men.

Ah, my friends, we say not one word against those who live upon the Atlantic coast, but the hardy pioneers who have braved all the dangers of the wilderness, who have made the desert to blossom as the rose—the pioneers away out there, who rear their children near to Nature's heart, where they can mingle their voices with the voices of the birds—out there where they have erected schoolhouses for the education of their young, churches where they

(Left) Glass whiskey flask with Republican "sound money" slogan; (Right) Glass candle lantern with acid-etched portraits of Bryan and Sewall.

praise their Creator, and cemeteries where rest the ashes of their dead—these people, we saw, are as deserving of the consideration of our party as any people in this country. It is for these that we speak. We do not come as aggressors. Our war is not a war of conquest; we are fighting in the defense of our homes, our families, and posterity. We have petitioned, and our petitions have been scorned; we have entreated, and our entreaties have been disregarded; we have begged, and they have mocked when our calamity came. We beg no longer; we entreat no more; we petition no more. We defy them.

The gentleman from Wisconsin has said that he fears a Robespierre. My friends, in this land of the free you need not fear that a tyrant will spring up from among the people. What we need is an Andrew Jackson to stand, as Jackson stood, against the encroachments of organized wealth.

They tell us that this platform was made to catch votes. We reply to them that changing conditions make new issues; that the principles upon which Democracy rests are as everlasting as the hills, but that they must be applied to new conditions as they arise. Conditions have arisen, and we are here to meet these conditions. They tell us that the income tax ought not to be brought in here; that it is a new idea. They criticize us for our criticism of the United States. My friends, we have not criticized; we have simply called attention to what you already know. If you want criticisms, read the dissenting opinions of the court. There you will find criticisms. They say that we passed an unconstitutional law; we deny it. The income tax was not unconstitutional when it was passed; it was not unconstitutional when it went before the Supreme Court for the first time; it did not become unconstitutional until one of the judges changed his mind, and we cannot be expected to know when a judge will change his mind. The income tax is just. It simply intends to put the burdens of government justly upon the backs of the people. I am in favor of an income tax. When I find a man who is not willing to bear his share of the burdens of the government which protects him, I find a man who is unworthy to enjoy the blessings of a government like ours.

They say that we are opposing national bank currency; it is true. If you read what Thomas Benton said, you will find he said that, in searching history, he could find but one parallel to Andrew Jackson; that was Cicero, who destroyed the conspiracy of Cataline and saved Rome. Benton said that Cicero only did for Rome what Jackson did for us when he destroyed the bank conspiracy and saved America. We say in our platform that we believe that the right to coin and issue money is a function of government. We believe it. We believe that it is a part of sovereignty, and can no more with safety be delegated to private individuals than we could afford to delegate to private individuals the power to make penal statutes or levy taxes. Mr. Jefferson, who was once regarded as good Democratic authority, seems to have differed in opinion from the gentleman who had addressed us on the part of the minority. Those who are opposed to this proposition tell us that the issue of paper money is a function of the bank, and that the Government ought to go out of the banking business. I stand with Jefferson rather than with them, and tell them, as he did, that the issue of money is a function of government, and that the banks ought to go out of the governing business.

They complain about the plank which declares against life tenure in office. They have tried to strain it to mean that which it does not mean. What we oppose by that plank is the life tenure which is being built up in Washington, and which excludes from participation in official benefits the humbler members of society.

Let me call your attention to two or three important things. The gentleman from New York says that he will propose an amendment to the platform providing that the proposed change in our monetary system shall not affect contracts already made. Let me remind you that there is no intention of affecting those contracts which according to present laws were made in gold; but if he means to say that we cannot change our monetary system without protecting those who have loaned money before the change was made, I desire to ask him where, in law or in morals, he can find justification for not

Desktop metal match holder. The wings, originally silver, lift.

protecting the debtors when the act of 1873 was passed, if he now insists that we must protect the creditors.

He says he will also propose an amendment which will provide for the suspension of free coinage if we fail to maintain the parity within a year. We reply that when we advocate a policy which we believe will be successful, we are not compelled to raise a doubt as to our own sincerity by suggesting what we shall do if we fail. I ask him, if he would apply his logic to us, why he does not apply it to himself. He says he wants this country to try to secure an international agreement. Why does he not tell us what he is going to do if he fails to secure an international agreement? There is more reason for him to do that than there is for us to provide against the failure to maintain the parity. Our opponents have tried for twenty years to secure an international agreement, and those are waiting for it most patiently who do not want it at all.

And now, my friends, let me come to the paramount issue. If they ask us why it is that we say more on the money question than we say upon the tariff question, I reply that, if protection has slain its thousands, the gold standard has slain its tens of thousands. If they ask us why we do not embody in our platform all the things that we believe in, we reply that when we have restored the money of the Constitution all necessary reforms will be possible; but that until this is done there is no other reform that can be accomplished.

Why is it that within three months such a change has come over the country? Three months ago, when it was confidently asserted that those who believe in the gold standard would frame our platform and nominate our candidates, even the advocates of the gold standard did not think that we could elect a President. And they had good reason for their doubt, because there is scarcely a State here to-day asking for the gold standard which is not in absolute control of the Republican Party. But note the change. Mr. McKinley was nominated at St. Louis upon a platform which declared for the maintenance of the gold standard until it can be changed into bimetallism by international agreement. Mr. McKinley was the most popular man among the Republicans, and three months ago everybody in the Republican Party prophesied his election. How is it to-day? Why, the man who was once pleased to think that he looked like Napoleon—that man shudders today when he remembers that he was nominated on the anniversary of the Battle of Waterloo. Not only that, but as he listens he can hear with ever-increasing distinctness the sound of the waves as they beat upon the lonely shores of St. Helena.

Why this change? Ah, my friends, is not the reason for the change evident to any one who will look at the matter? No private character, however pure, no personal popularity, however great, can protect from the avenging wrath of an indignant people a man who will declare that he is in favor of fastening the gold standard upon this country, or who is willing to surrender the right of self-government and place the legislative control of our affairs in the hands of foreign potentates and powers.

We go forth confident that we shall win. Why? Because upon the paramount issue of this campaign there is not a spot of ground upon which the enemy will dare to challenge battle. If they tell us that the gold standard is a good thing, we shall point to their platform and tell them that their platform pledges the party to get rid of the gold standard and substitute bimetallism. If the gold standard is a good thing, why try to get rid of it? I call your attention to the fact that some of the very people who are in this convention today and who tell us that we ought to declare in favor of international bimetallism—thereby declaring that the gold standard is wrong and that the principle of bimetallism is better—these very people four months ago were open and avowed advocates of the gold standard, and were then telling us that we could not legislate two metals together, even with the aid of all the world. If the gold standard is a good thing, we ought to declare in favor of its retention and not in favor of abandoning it; and if the old standard is a bad thing why should we wait until other nations are willing to help us to let go? Here is the line of battle, and we care not upon which issue they force the fight; we are prepared to meet them on either issue or on both. If they tell us that the gold standard is the standard of civilization, we reply to them that this, the most enlightened of all the nations of the earth, has never declared for a gold standard and that both the great parties of the year are declaring against it. If the gold standard is the standard of civilization, why, my friends, should we not have it? If they come to meet us on that issue we can present the history of our nation. More than that; we can tell them that they will search the pages of history in vain to find a single instance where the common people of any land have ever declared themselves in favor of the gold standard. They can find where the holders of fixed investments have declared for a gold standard, but not where the masses have.

Mr. Carlisle said in 1878 that this was a struggle between "the idle holders of idle capital" and "the struggling masses, who produce the wealth and pay the taxes of the country"; and, my friends, the question we are to decide is: Upon which side will the Democratic Party fight; upon the side of "the idle holders of idle capital" or upon the side of "the struggling masses?" That is the question which the party must answer first, and then it must be answered by each individual hereafter. The sympathies of the Democratic Party, as shown by the platform, are on the side of the struggling masses who have ever been the foundation of the Democratic Party. There are two ideas of government.

During 1895 and early 1896, pro-silver forces had been taking control of the Democratic Party from President Grover Cleveland's supporters. Now, their task was to find a spokesman for their cause. The more prominent figures were not inspiring: Congressman Richard Bland of Missouri—known to both friends and opponents as "Silver Dick"—stirred little enthusiasm—and Governor Horace Boies of Iowa was only a lukewarm silver supporter. The situation was ripe for a newcomer to emerge as the free-silver champion.

On the second evening of the convention, William Jennings Bryan, an Omaha editor and former congressman from Nebraska, rose to defend the silver plank of the platform. Before he finished speaking, the assembled delegates knew that they had found a leader. In a stirring address, the thirty-six-year-old Bryan thrilled his listeners as he defended silver. His words rang out in an electrifying challenge:

> You come to us and tell us that the great cities are in favor of the gold standard. We reply that the great cities rest upon our broad and fertile prairies. Burn down your cities and leave our farms, and your cities will spring up again as if by magic; but destroy our farms, and the grass will grow in the streets of every city in the country.

And, to the half-hysterical audience, he concluded with the rousing peroration:

> Having behind us the producing masses of this nation and the world, the laboring interests, and the tailors everywhere, we will answer their demand for a gold standard by saying to them: You shall not press down upon the brow of labor this crown of thorns—you shall not crucify mankind upon a cross of gold!

The tumult that followed, one observer recorded, "was like that of a great sea thundering against the dikes. Twenty thousand men and women went mad with an irresistible enthusiasm." On the fifth ballot, they acclaimed Bryan the nominee of the Democratic Party.

There are those who believe that, if you will only legislate to make the well-to-do prosperous, their prosperity will leak through on those below. The Democratic idea, however, has been that if you legislate to make the masses prosperous, their prosperity will find its way up through every class which rests upon them.

You come to us and tell us that the great cities are in favor of the gold standard; we reply that the great cities rest upon our broad and fertile prairies. Burn down your cities and leave our farms, and your cities will spring up again as if by magic; but destroy our farms and the grass will grow in the streets of every city in the country.

My friends, we declare that this nation is able to legislate for its own people on every question, without waiting for the aid or consent of every other nation on earth; and upon that issue we expect to carry every State in the Union. I shall not slander the inhabitants of the fair state of Massachusetts nor the inhabitants of the fair state of New York by saying that, when they are confronted with the proposition, they will declare that this nation is not able to attend to its own business. It is the issue of 1776 over again. Our ancestors, when but three millions in number, had the courage to declare their political independence of every other nation; shall we, their descendants, when we have grown to seventy millions, declare that we are less independent than our forefathers? No, my friends, that will never be the verdict of our people. Therefore, we care not upon what lines the battle is fought. If they say bimetallism is good, but that we cannot have it until other nations help us, we reply that, instead of having a gold standard because England has, we will restore bimetallism, and then let England have bimetallism because the United States has it. If they dare to come out in the open field and defend the gold standard as a good thing, we will fight them to the uttermost. Having behind us the producing masses of this nation and the world, supported by the commercial interests, the laboring interests, and the toilers everywhere, we will answer their demand for a gold standard by saying no to them: You shall not press down upon the brow of labor this crown of thorns—you shall not crucify mankind upon a cross of gold.

Bryan Becomes Populist Candidate

Senator William V. Allen of Nebraska was acclaimed as "the intellectual giant of Populism." Allen distinguished himself early in his senatorial career by speaking continuously for fifteen hours during a filibuster against the repeal of the Sherman Silver Purchase Act (1893). His speech did not prevent repeal but he emerged as a leader of the pro-silver forces. In 1896, he was one of those Populist leaders who favored fusion with the Democrats. As chairman of the nominating committee, he did much to further that end by offering Bryan the party's nomination. Allen explained that the Populists did not expect Bryan to follow their platform other than the "free silver" plank.

At a Convention of the People's Party held at St. Louis from July 22 to 25 of the current year, you were unanimously nominated for President of the United States to be voted for at the approaching general election. It was known at the time that you had been nominated by the Democratic Party [. . .] and that you would in all probability accept the same in a formal manner. Your nomination by the People's Party was not, therefore, made with any thought that you were a Populist, or that you accepted all the doctrines declared by the St. Louis platform. It was due largely to the fact that the money question is the overshadowing political issue of the age, and because you have at all times been an unswerving, able and fearless advocate of the free and unlimited coinage of silver and gold on terms of equality at the mints of the United States at the ratio of 16 to 1. It was thought also that the observance of a patriotic duty required a union of all reform forces, and the Convention took the liberty, without soliciting or consulting you, of placing your name before the people as its standard-bearer.

The Convention was, in doing so, guided by deep solicitude for the common welfare and acting on its own motion, prompted alone by a desire to bring about the best attainable results. [. . .] You will observe by the closing language of the St. Louis platform that the Convention recognized the money question as the great issue of the day, and because Populists believed that you are in accord with them on this question you will receive their ballots in November.

It has at no time been expected, or is it now, that you will abandon your adhesion to the Chicago platform nor that you will accept all that is desired by the People's Party platform, however more gratifying that would be to all Populists. It must be understood that the party does not abate one jot or tittle of loyalty to its principles. We have declared ourselves in favor of many important reforms and go further than you or your

Celluloid campaign button with a Bryan caricature. The celluloid pinback button was patented prior to the 1896 campaign.

party have gone. These reforms are in our judgment essential to the liberation of the people from present unjust and iniquitous industrial bondage.

In accordance with the precedent of our party, we take this method of notifying you of your nomination. [. . .] In sending this letter of notification of the great honor that has justly been conferred on you by your party, it is needless for us to assure you that you have the confidence and esteem of all. Your splendid abilities, known integrity, competency and eminent fitness for the position justly entitle you to a high rank among the great statesmen of the Nation.

We feel that in the event of your election, which now seems certain, you will carry into execution the principles of monetary reform to the end that the people shall enjoy better industrial conditions. It is not anticipated that this can be done with undue haste, but that it will be done gradually and in a way to infuse confidence and hope of better conditions for all.

Mechanical advertisement cards. The wheel turns to show "the people's choice."

Campaign sheet music.

The People's Party will exact of you no promise further than those made in your public utterances and exemplified in a life devoted to the welfare of the race: nor will we ask you to abandon the party of which you are an honored member. In your nomination our party has risen above mere partisan surroundings, adopting a high plane of patriotism, believing that a division of forces would result in the election of William McKinley, the foremost advocate of a deeply burdensome and unnatural taxation and the criminal policy of the single gold standard, resulting ultimately, if not in some manner checked, in the complete destruction and disintegration of our form of government.

Your elevation to the Chief Magistracy of the Nation would be regarded as a vindication of the right of the people to govern, and we entertain no doubt that you will prove a worthy successor of the immortal Jefferson and Lincoln, and that your public life, like theirs, will illustrate the purity and loftiness of American statesmanship. [. . .]

We have the honor to be your most obedient servants.

★ McKinley Accepts the Nomination ★

What we now know as acceptance speeches at party conventions were originally letters dispatched by the nominated candidate in response to a letter notifying him of the offered honor. In 1852, Franklin Pierce was notified in person by a delegation sent from the convention. With representatives of the party and the candidate now in one place, a formal ceremony could occur. Typically such ceremonies took place six weeks to two months after the convention. On August 26, 1896, a formal delegation appointed by the Republican convention notified William McKinley of his nomination. From the porch of his home at Canton, Ohio, McKinley delivered the following acceptance speech.

In pursuance of the promise made to your committee when notified of my nomination as the Republican candidate for President, I beg to submit this formal acceptance of that high honor, and to consider in detail questions at issue in the pending campaign. [. . .]

For the first time since 1868, if ever before, there is presented to the American people this year a clear and direct issue as to our monetary system, of vast importance in its effects, and upon the right settlement of which rests largely the financial honor and prosperity of the country. It is proposed by one wing of the Democratic Party and its allies, the People's and Silver parties, to inaugurate the free and unlimited coinage of silver by independent action on the part of the United States at a ratio of 16 ounces of silver to 1 ounce of gold.

The mere declaration of this purpose is a menace to our financial and industrial interests, and has already created universal alarm. It involves great peril to the credit and business of the country, a peril so grace that conservative men everywhere are breaking away from their old party associations and uniting with other patriotic citizens in emphatic protest against the platform of the Democratic National Convention as an assault upon the faith and honor of the Government and the welfare of the people. We have had few questions in the lifetime of the Republic more serious than the one which is thus presented.

The character of the money which shall measure our values and exchanges and settle our balances with one another and with the nations of the world is of such primary importance and so far-reaching in its consequences as to call for the most painstaking investigation, and, in the end a sober and unprejudiced judgment at the polls.

We must not be misled by phrases, nor deluded by false theories. Free silver would not mean that silver dollars were to be freely had without cost of labor. It would mean that the free use of the mints of the United

States for the few who are owners of silver bullion, but would make silver coin no freer to the many who are engaged in other enterprises. It would not make labor easier, the hours of labor shorter, or the pay better. It would not make farming less laborious, or more profitable. It would create no new occupations. It would add nothing to the comfort of the masses, the capital of the people, or the wealth of the Nation. It seeks to introduce a new measure of value, but would add no value to the thing measured. It would not conserve values. On the contrary, it would derange all existing values. It would not restore business confidence, but its direct effect would by to destroy the little which yet remains.

⚜⚜⚜⚜⚜

We have coined since 1878 more than 400,000,000 of silver dollars, which are maintained by the Government at parity with gold and are a full legal tender for the payment of all debts public and private. How are the silver dollars now in use different from those which would be in use under free coinage? They are to be of the same weight and fineness; they are to bear the same stamp of the Government. Why would they not be of the same value? I answer: The silver dollars now in use were coined on account of the Government and not for private account or gain, and the Government has solemnly agreed to keep them as good as the best dollars we have. The Government bought the silver bullion at its market value and coined it into silver dollars. Having exclusive control of the mintage, it only coins what it can hold at a parity with gold. The profit, representing the difference between the commercial value of the silver bullion and the face value of the silver dollar, goes to the Government for the benefit of the people.

The Government bought the silver bullion contained in the silver dollar at very much less than its coinage value. It paid it out to the creditors and put it in circulation among the people at its face value of 100 cents, or a full dollar. It required the people to accept it as legal tender, and is thus morally bound to maintain it at a parity with gold, which was then, as now, the recognized standard with us and the most enlightened nations of the world. The Government having issued and circulated the silver dollar, it must in honor protect the holder from loss. This obligation it has so far sacredly kept. Not only is there a moral obligation, but there is a legal obligation expressed in public statute to maintain the parity.

These dollars, in the particulars I have named, are not the same as the dollars which would be issued under free coinage. They would be the same in form, but different in value. The Government would have no part of the profit. It would take upon itself no obligation. It would not put the dollars into circulation. It could only get them, as any citizen would get them, by giving something for them. It would deliver them to those who deposited the silver, and its connection with the transaction there ends.

Such are the silver dollars which would be issued under free coinage of silver at a ratio of 16 to 1. Who would then maintain the parity? What would keep them at a par with gold? There would be no obligation resting upon the Government to do it, and if there were, it would be powerless to do it. The simple truth is, we would be driven to a silver basis—to silver monometallism. These dollars, therefore, would stand upon their real value. If the free and unlimited coinage of silver, at a ratio of 16 ounces of silver to 1 ounce of gold, would, as some of its advocates assert, make 53 cents in silver worth 100 cents, and the silver dollar equal to the gold dollar, then we would have no cheaper more than now, and it would be no easier to get. But that such would be the result is against reason and is contradicted by experience in all times and in all lands. It means the debasement of our currency to the amount of the difference between the commercial and coin value of the silver dollar, which is ever changing, and the effect would be to reduce property values, entail untold financial loss, destroy confidence, impair the obligations of existing contracts, further impoverish the laborers and producers of the country, create a panic of unparalleled severity and inflict upon trade and commerce a deadly blow. Against any such policy I am unalterably opposed.

Bimetallism cannot be secured by independent action on our part. It cannot be obtained by opening our mints to the unlimited coinage of the silver of the world, at a ratio of 16 ounces of silver to 1 ounce of gold, when the commercial ratio is more than 30 ounces of silver to 1 ounce of gold. Mexico and China have tried the experiment. Mexico has free coinage of silver and gold at a ratio slightly in excess of 16 1/2 ounces of silver to 1 ounce of gold, and while her mints are freely open to both metals at that ratio, not a single dollar in gold bullion is coined and circulated as money. Gold has been driven out of circulation in those countries, and they are on a silver basis alone. Until international agreement is had it is the plain duty of the United States to maintain the gold standard.

※※※※※

The Republican Party has not been, and is not now, opposed to the use of silver money, as its record abundantly shows. It has done all that could be done for its increased use, with safety and honor, by the United States acting apart from other Governments. There are those who think that it has already gone beyond the limit of financial prudence. Surely we can go no further, and we must not permit false lights to lure us across the danger line.

※※※※※

It is not proposed by the Republican Party to take from the circulating medium of the country any of the silver we now have. On the contrary, it is proposed to keep all of the silver money now in circulation on a parity with gold by maintaining the pledge of the Government that all of it shall be equal to gold. This has been the unbroken policy of the Republican Party since 1878. It has inaugurated no new policy. It will keep in circulation and as good as gold all of the silver and paper money which is not included in the currency of the country. It will maintain their parity. It will preserve their equality in the future, as it has always done in the past. It will not consent to put this country on a silver basis, which would inevitably follow independent free coinage at a ratio of 16 to 1. It will oppose the expulsion of gold from our circulation.

If there is any one thing that should be free from speculation and fluctuation it is the money of a country. It ought never to be the subject of mere partisan contention. When we part with our labor, our products, or our property, we should receive in return money which is as stable and unchanging in value as the ingenuity of honest men can make it. Debasement of the currency means destruction of values. No one suffers so much from cheap money as the farmers and laborers. They are the first to feel its bad effects and the last to recover from them. This has been the uniform experience of all countries, and here, as elsewhere, the poor, and not the rich, are always the greatest sufferers from every attempt to debase our money. It would fall with alarming severity upon investments already made; upon insurance companies and their policy-holders; upon savings banks and their depositors; upon building and loan associations and their members; upon the savings of thrift; upon pensioners and their families, and upon wage-earners and the purchasing power of their wages.

⚬⚬⚬⚬⚬

It is a cause for painful regret and solicitude that an effort is being made by those high in the counsels of the allied parties to divide the people of this country into classes and create distinctions among us which, in fact, do not exist and are repugnant to our form of government. These appeals to passion and prejudice are beneath the spirit and intelligence of a free people and should be met with stern rebuke by those they are sought to influence, and I believe they will be. Every attempt to array class against class, "the classes against the masses," section against section, labor against capital, "the poor against the rich," or interest against interest in the United States, is in the highest degree reprehensible. It is opposed to the National instinct and interest, and should be resisted by every citizen.

We are not a Nation of classes, but of sturdy, free, independent and honorable people despising the demagogue and never capitulating to dishonor. This ever-recurring effort endangers popular government and is a menace to our liberties. It is not a new campaign device or party appeal. It is as old as government among men, but was never more untimely and unfortunate than now.

⚜⚜⚜⚜

Another issue of supreme importance is that of protection. The peril of free silver is a menace to be feared; we are already experiencing the effect of partial free trade. The one must be averted; the other corrected. The Republican Party is wedded to the doctrine of protection, and was never more earnest in its support and advocacy than now. If argument were needed to strengthen or increase the hold of that system on the party and people it is found in the lesson and experience of the last three years. Men realize in their own daily lives what before was to many of them only report, history or tradition. They have had a trial of both systems, and know what each has done for them. [. . .]

⚜⚜⚜⚜

It is a mere pretense to attribute the hard times to the fact that all currency is on a gold basis. Good money never made times hard. Those who assert that our present industrial and financial depression is the result of the gold standard have not read American history aright or been careful students of the events of recent years. We never had greater prosperity in this country, in every field of employment and industry, than in the busy years from 1880 to 1892, during all of which time this country was on a gold basis and employed more gold money in its fiscal and business operations than ever before.

We had, too, a protective tariff under which ample revenues were collected for the Government, and an accumulating surplus, which was constantly applied to the payment of the public debt. Let us hold fast to that which we know is good. It is not more money we want; what we want it to put the money we already have at work. When money is employed, men are employed. Both have always been steadily and remuneratively engaged during all the years of protective tariff legislation. When those who have money lack confidence in the stability of values and investments, they will not part with their money. Business is stagnated—the life-blood of trade is checked and congested. We cannot restore the public confidence by an act which would revolutionize all

Miniature sample of a street banner.

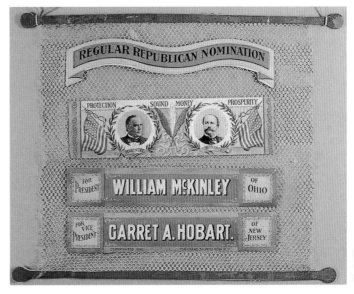

values, or an act which entails a deficiency in the public revenue. We cannot inspire confidence by advocating repudiation or practicing dishonesty. We cannot restore confidence, either to the Treasury or to the people, with a change in our present tariff legislation.

The only measure of a general nature that affected the Treasury and the employments of our people passed by the 53rd Congress was the General Tariff act, which did not receive the approval of the President. Whatever virtues may be claimed for that act, there is confessedly one which it does not possess. It lacks the essential virtue of its creation—the raising of revenue sufficient to supply the needs of the Government. It has at no time provided enough revenue for such needs, but it has caused a constant deficiency in the Treasury and a steady depletion in the earnings of labor and land. It has contributed to swell our National debt more than $262,000,000, a sum nearly as great as the debt of the Government from Washington to Lincoln, including all our foreign wars from the Revolution to the Rebellion. Since its passage, work at home has been diminished; prices of agricultural products have fallen; confidence has been arrested, and general business demoralization is seen on every hand.

❦❦❦❦❦

[. . .] It is not an increase in the volume of money which is the need of the time, but an increase in the volume of business. Not an increase of coin, but an increase of confidence. Not more coinage, but a more active use of the money coined. Not open mints for the unlimited coinage of the silver of the world, but open mills for the full and unrestricted labor of American working-men. The employment of our mints for the coinage of the silver of the world would not bring the necessaries and comforts of life back to our people. This will only come with the employment of the masses, and such employment is certain to follow the re-establishment of a wise protective policy which shall encourage manufacturing at home.

Protection has lost none of its virtue and importance. The first duty of the Republican Party, if restored to power in the country, will be the enactment of a tariff law which will raise all the money necessary to conduct the Government, economically and honestly administered, and so adjusted as to give preference to home manufacturers and adequate protection to home labor and the home market. We are not committed to any special schedules or rates of duty are imposed remains the same. Our duties should always be high enough to measure the difference between the wages paid labor at home and in competing countries, and to adequately protect American investments and American enterprises.

Our farmers have been hurt by the changes in our tariff legislation as severely as our laborers and manufacturers, badly as they have suffered. The Republican platform wisely declares in favor of such encouragement to our sugar interests "as will lead to the production on American soil of all the sugar which the American people use." It promises to our wool and woolen interests "the most ample protection," a guaranty that ought to commend itself to every patriotic citizen. Never was a more grievous wrong done the farmers of our country than that so unjustly inflicted during the last three years upon the wool-growers of America. Although among our most industrious and useful citizens, their interests have been practically destroyed, and our woolen man-ufacturers involved in similar disaster. At no time within the last thirty-six years and perhaps never during any previous period, have so many of our woolen factories been suspended as now. The Republican Party can be relied upon to correct these great wrongs if again intrusted with the control of Congress. [. . .]

❧❧❧❧❧

The pledge of the Republican National Convention that our civil service laws "shall be sustained and thoroughly and honestly enforced, and extended wherever practicable," is in keeping with the position of the party for the last twenty-four years, and will be faithfully observed. Our opponents decry these reforms. They appear willing to abandon all the advantages gained, after so many years' agitation and effort. They encourage a return to methods of party favoritism which both parties have often denounced, that experience has condemned, and that the people have repeatedly disapproved. The Republican Party earnestly opposes this reactionary and entirely unjustifiable policy. It will take no backward step upon this question. It will seek to improve, but never degrade, the public service.

There are other important and timely declarations in the platform which I cannot here discuss. I must content myself with saying that they have my approval. [. . .]

We avoid no issues. We meet the sudden, dangerous and revolutionary assault upon law and order, and upon those to whom is confided by the Constitution and laws the authority to uphold and maintain them, which our opponents have made, with the same courage that we have faced every emergency since our organization as a party, more than forty years ago. Government by law must first be assured; everything else can wait. The spirit of lawlessness must be extinguished by the fires of an unselfish and lofty patriotism. Every attack upon the public faith and every suggestion of the repudiation of debts, public or private, must be rebuked by all men who believe that honesty is the best policy, or who love their country and would preserve unsullied its National honor.

McKinley's First Inaugural Address

On March 4, 1897, Republican clubs from all parts of America descended on Washington to witness William McKinley's inauguration. As the President unfolded his manuscript and put on his reading glasses, he could see a placard in the distance boldly proclaiming: "God saved US from Bryan." McKinley's inauguration is the first for which we have an audio and visual record: it was recorded by Thomas Edison's new motion picture camera and Gramophone.

In obedience to the will of the people, and in their presence, by the authority vested in me by this oath, I assume the arduous and responsible duties of President of the United States, relying upon the support of my countrymen and invoking the guidance of Almighty God. [. . .]

The responsibilities of the high trust to which I have been called—always of grave importance—are augmented by the prevailing business conditions entailing idleness upon willing labor and loss to useful enterprises. The country is suffering from industrial disturbances from which speedy relief must be had. Our financial system needs some revision; our money is all good now, but its value must not further be threatened. It should all be put upon an enduring basis, not subject to easy attack, nor its stability to doubt or dispute. Our currency should continue under the supervision of the Government. The several forms of our paper money offer, in my judgment, a constant embarrassment to the Government and a safe balance in the Treasury. Therefore I believe it necessary to devise a system which, without diminishing the circulating medium or offering a premium for its contraction, will present a remedy for those arrangements which, temporary in their nature, might well in the years of our prosperity have been displaced by wiser provisions. With adequate revenue secured, but not until then, we can enter upon such changes in our fiscal laws as will, while insuring safety and volume to our money, no longer impose upon the Government the necessity of maintaining so large a gold reserve, with its attendant and inevitable temptations to speculation. Most of our financial laws are the outgrowth of experience and trial, and should not be amended without investigation and demonstration of the wisdom of the proposed changes. We must be both "sure we are right" and "make haste slowly." If, therefore, Congress, in its wisdom, shall deem it expedient to create a commission to take under early consideration the revision of our coinage, banking and currency laws, and give them that exhaustive, careful and dispassionate examination that their importance demands, I shall cordially concur in such action. If such power is vested in the President, it is my purpose to appoint a commission of prominent, well-informed citizens of different parties, who will command public confidence, both on account of their ability and special fitness for the work. Business experience and public training may thus be combined, and the patriotic zeal of the friends of the country be so directed that such a report will be made as to receive the support of all parties, and our finances cease to be the subject of mere partisan contention. The experiment is, at all events, worth a trial, and, in my opinion, it can but prove beneficial to the entire country.

The question of international bimetallism will have early and earnest attention. It will be my constant endeavor to secure it by co-operation with the other great commercial powers of the world. Until that condition is realized when the parity between our gold and silver money springs from and is supported by the relative value of the two metals, the value of the silver already coined and of that which may hereafter be coined, must be kept constantly at par with gold by every resource at our command. The credit of the Government, the integrity of its currency, and the inviolability of its obligations must be preserved. This was the commanding verdict of the people, and it will not be unheeded.

Economy is demanded in every branch of the Government at all times, but especially in periods, like the present, of depression in business and distress among the people. The severest economy must be observed in all public expenditures, and extravagance stopped wherever it is found, and prevented wherever in the future it may be developed. If the revenues are to remain as now, the only relief that can come must be from decreased expenditures. But the present must not become the permanent condition of the Government. It has been our uniform practice to retire, not increase our outstanding obligations, and this policy must again be resumed and vigorously enforced. Our revenues should always be large enough to meet with ease and

Silk flag banner of McKinley and Hobart.

promptness not only our current needs and the principal and interest of the public debt, but to make proper and liberal provision for that most deserving body of public creditors, the soldiers and sailors and the widows and orphans who are the pensioners of the United States.

The Government should not be permitted to run behind or increase its debt in times like the present. Suitably to provide against this is the mandate of duty—the certain and easy remedy for most of our financial difficulties. A deficiency is inevitable so long as the expenditures of the Government exceed its receipts. It can only be met by loans or an increased revenue. While a large annual surplus of revenue may invite waste and extravagance, inadequate revenue creates distrust and undermines public and private credit. Neither should be encouraged. Between more loans and more revenue there ought to be but one opinion. We should have more revenue, and that without delay, hindrance, or postponement. A surplus in the Treasury created by loans is not a permanent or safe reliance. It will suffice while it lasts, but it can not last long while the outlays of the Government are greater than its receipts, as has been the case during the past two years. Nor must it be forgotten that however much such loans may temporarily relieve the situation, the Government is still indebted for the amount of the surplus thus accrued, which it must ultimately pay, while its ability to pay is not strengthened, but weakened by a continued deficit. Loans are imperative in great emergencies to preserve the Government or its credit, but a failure to supply needed revenue in time of peace for the maintenance of either has no justification.

The best way for the Government to maintain its credit is to pay as it goes—not by resorting to loans, but by keeping out of debt—through an adequate income secured by a system of taxation, external or internal, or both. It is the settled policy of the Government, pursued from the beginning and practiced by all parties and Administrations, to raise the bulk of our revenue from taxes upon foreign productions entering the United States for sale and consumption, and avoiding, for the most part, every form of direct taxation, except in time of war. The country is clearly opposed to any needless additions to the subject of internal taxation, and is committed by its latest popular utterance to the system of tariff taxation. There can be no misunderstanding, either, about the principle upon which this tariff taxation shall be levied. Nothing has ever been made plainer at a general election than that the controlling principle in the raising of revenue from duties on imports is zealous care for American interests and American labor. The people have declared that such legislation should be had as will give ample protection and encouragement to the industries and the development of our country. It is, therefore, earnestly hoped and expected that Congress will, at the earliest practicable moment, enact revenue legislation that shall be fair, reasonable,

Wooden gold key. An inaugural souvenir sold in Washington, D.C.

conservative, and just, and which, while supplying sufficient revenue for public purposes, will still be signally beneficial and helpful to every section and every enterprise of the people. To this policy we are all, of whatever party, firmly bound by the voice of the people—a power vastly more potential than the expression of any political platform. [. . .]

The depression of the past four years has fallen with especial severity upon the great body of toilers of the country, and upon none more than the holders of small farms. Agriculture has languished and labor suffered. The revival of manufacturing will be a relief to both. No portion of our population is more devoted to the institution of free government nor more loyal in their support, while none bears more cheerfully or fully its proper share in the maintenance of the Government or is better entitled to its wise and liberal care and protection. Legislation helpful to producers is beneficial to all. The depressed condition of industry on the farm and in the mine and factory has lessened the ability of the people to meet the demands upon them, and they rightfully expect that not only a system of revenue shall be established that will secure the largest income with the least burden, but that every means will be taken to decrease, rather than increase, our public expenditures. Business conditions are not the most promising. It will take time to restore the prosperity of former years. If we cannot promptly attain it, we can resolutely turn our faces in that direction and aid its return by friendly legislation. However troublesome the situation may appear, Congress will not, I am sure, be found lacking in disposition or ability to relieve it as far as legislation can do so. The restoration of confidence and the revival of business, which men of all parties so much desire, depend more largely upon the prompt, energetic, and intelligent action of Congress than upon any other single agency affecting the situation. [. . .]

One of the lessons taught by the late election, which all can rejoice in, is that the citizens of the United States are both law-respecting and law-abiding people, not easily swerved from the path of patriotism and honor. This is in entire accord with the genius of our institutions, and but emphasizes the advantages of inculcating even a greater love for law and order in the future. Immunity should be granted to none who violate the laws, whether individuals, corporations, or communities; and as the Constitution imposes upon the President the duty of both its own execution, and of the statutes enacted in pursuance of its provisions, I shall endeavor carefully to carry them into effect. The declaration of the party now restored to power has been in the past that of "opposition to all combinations of capital organized in trusts, or otherwise, to control arbitrarily the condition of trade among our citizens," and it has supported "such legislation as will prevent the execution of all schemes to oppress the people by undue charges on their supplies, or by unjust rates for the transportation of their products to the market." This purpose will be steadily pursued, both by the enforcement of the laws now in existence and the recommendation and support of such new statutes as may be necessary to carry it into effect. [. . .]

Reforms in the civil service must go on; but the changes should be real and genuine, not perfunctory, or prompted by a zeal in behalf of any party simply because it happens to be in power. As a member of Congress I voted and spoke in favor of the present law, and I shall attempt its enforcement in the spirit in which it was enacted. The purpose in view was to secure the most efficient service of the best men who would accept appointment under the Government, retaining faithful and devoted public servants in office, but shielding none, under the authority of any rule or custom, who are inefficient, incompetent, or unworthy. The best interests of the country demand this, and the people heartily approve the law wherever and whenever it has been thus administrated.

Congress should give prompt attention to the restoration of our American merchant marine, once the pride of the seas in all the great ocean highways of commerce. To my mind, few more important subjects so imperatively demand its intelligent consideration. The United States has progressed with marvelous rapidity in every field of enterprise and endeavor until we have become foremost in nearly all the great lines of inland trade, commerce, and industry. Yet, while this is true, our American merchant marine has been steadily declining until it is now lower, both in the percentage of tonnage and the number of vessels employed, than it was prior to the Civil War. Commendable progress has been made of late years in the upbuilding of the American Navy, but we must supplement these efforts by providing as a proper consort for it a merchant marine amply sufficient for our own carrying trade to foreign countries. The question is one that appeals both to our business necessities and the patriotic aspirations of a great people.

Metal matchsafes with McKinley and Bryan.

It has been the policy of the United States since the foundation of the Government to cultivate relations of peace and amity with all the nations of the world, and this accords with my conception of our duty now. We have cherished the policy of non-interference with affairs of foreign governments wisely inaugurated by Washington, keeping ourselves free from entanglement, either as allies or foes, content to leave undisturbed with them the settlement of their own domestic concerns. It will be our aim to pursue a firm and dignified foreign policy, which shall be just, impartial, ever watchful of our national honor, and always insisting upon the enforcement of the lawful rights of American citizens everywhere. Our diplomacy should seek nothing more and accept nothing less than is due us. We want no wars of conquest; we must avoid the temptation of territorial aggression. War should never be entered upon until every agency of peace has failed; peace is preferable to war in almost every contingency. Arbitration is the true method of settlement of international as well as local or individual differences. It was recognized as the best means of

The Union League were patriotic organizations during the Civil War. After the war, they became social and political groups, invariably backing Republican candidates.

adjustment of differences between employers and employees by the Forty-ninth Congress, in 1886, and its application was extended to our diplomatic relations by the unanimous concurrence of the Senate and House of the Fifty-first Congress in 1890. The latter resolution was accepted as the basis of negotiations with us by the British House of Commons in 1893, and upon our invitation a treaty of arbitration between the United States and Great Britain was signed at Washington and transmitted to the Senate for its ratification in January last. Since this treaty is clearly the result of our own initiative; since it has been recognized as the leading feature of our foreign policy throughout our entire national history—the adjustment of difficulties by judicial methods rather than force of arms—and since it presents to the world the glorious example of reason and peace, not passion and war, controlling the relations between two of the greatest nations in the world, an example certain to be followed by others, I respectfully urge the early action of the Senate thereon, not merely as a matter of policy, but as a duty to mankind. The importance and moral influence of the ratification of such a treaty can hardly be overestimated in the cause of advancing civilization. It may well engage the best thought of the statesmen and people of every country, and I cannot but consider it fortunate that it was reserved to the United States to have the leadership in so grand a work. [. . .]

In conclusion, I congratulate the country upon the fraternal spirit of the people and the manifestations of good will everywhere so apparent. The recent election not only most fortunately demonstrated the obliteration of sectional or geographical lines, but to some extent also the prejudices which for years have distracted our councils and marred our true greatness as a nation. The triumph of the people, whose verdict is carried into effect today, is not the triumph of one section, nor wholly of one party, but of all sections and all the people. The North and the South no longer divide on the old lines, but upon principles and policies; and in this fact surely every lover of the country can find cause for true felicitation.

Let us rejoice in and cultivate this spirit; it is ennobling and will be both a gain and a blessing to our beloved country. It will be my constant aim to do nothing, and permit nothing to be done, that will arrest or disturb this growing sentiment of unity and cooperation, this revival of esteem and affiliation which now animates so many thousands in both the old antagonistic sections, but I shall cheerfully do everything possible to promote and increase it. Let me again repeat the words of the oath administered by the Chief Justice which, in their respective spheres, so far as applicable, I would have all my countrymen observe: "I will faithfully execute the office of President of the United States, and will, to the best of my ability, preserve, protect, and defend the Constitution of the United States." This is the obligation I have reverently taken before the Lord Most High. To keep it will be my single purpose, my constant prayer; and I shall confidently rely upon the forbearance and assistance of all the people in the discharge of my solemn responsibilities.

The Annexation of Hawaii

On January 17, 1893, an American-supported coup overthrew Hawaiian Queen Liliuokalani and established the Republic of Hawaii. Sanford B. Dole, the Hawaiian-born son of American missionaries, headed the new government. When President Grover Cleveland received word of the revolution and the use of some 300 marines, he, like the Hawaiian queen, reacted with indignation and incredulity. Cleveland sought the reinstatement of the queen but Dole and his associates refused to surrender power. Queen Liliuokalani went to Washington to plead her case. But, the United States was now pursuing an imperialist policy of "manifest destiny." The timing of a "Hawaii for Hawaiians" argument was bad. Congressional expansionists cared little about such native slogans.

In July 1898, President William McKinley formally authorized American annexation of the Republic of Hawaii. Congress followed with this treaty. McKinley appointed Dole the first governor. No longer a curious Polynesian kingdom in the middle of the Pacific Ocean, Hawaii was now a possession of the powerful United States. Former President Cleveland wrote that he was "ashamed of the whole affair" and ex-Queen Liliuokalani compared the plight of her 150,000 subjects to that of America's original Indian inhabitants.

Whereas, the Government of the Republic of Hawaii having, in due form, signified its consent, in the manner provided by its constitution, to cede absolutely and without reserve to the United States of America, all rights of sovereignty of whatsoever kind in and over the Hawaiian Islands and their dependencies, and also to cede and transfer to the United States, the absolute fee and ownership of all public, Government, or Crown lands, public buildings or edifices, ports, harbors, military equipment, and all other public property of every kind and description belonging to the Government of the Hawaiian Islands, together with every right and appurtenance thereunto appertaining: Therefore,

Resolved by the Senate and House of Representatives of the United States of America in Congress assembled, That said cession is accepted, ratified, and confirmed, and that the said Hawaiian Islands and their dependencies be, and they are hereby, annexed as a part of the territory of the United States and are subject to the sovereign dominion thereof, and that all and singular the property and rights hereinbefore mentioned are vested in the United States of America.

The existing laws of the United States relative to public lands shall not apply to such lands in the Hawaiian Islands; but the Congress of the United States shall enact special laws for their management and disposition: Provided, That all revenue from or proceeds of the same, except as regards such part thereof as may be used or occupied for the civil, military, or naval purposes of the United States, or may be assigned for the use of the local government, shall be used solely for the benefit of the inhabitants of the Hawaiian Islands for educational and other public purposes.

Until Congress shall provide for the government of such islands all the civil, judicial, and military powers exercised by the officers of the existing government in said islands shall be vested in such person or persons and

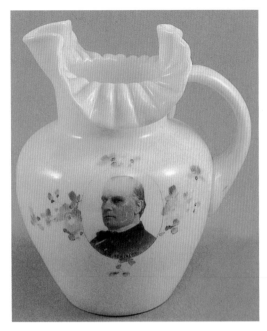

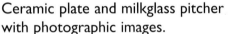

Ceramic plate and milkglass pitcher
with photographic images.

shall be exercised in such manner as the President of the United States shall direct; and the President shall have power to remove said officers and fill the vacancies so occasioned.

The existing treaties of the Hawaiian Islands with foreign nations shall forthwith cease and determine, being replaced by such treaties as may exist, or as may be hereafter concluded, between the United States and such foreign nations. The municipal legislation of the Hawaiian Islands, not enacted for the fulfillment of the treaties so extinguished, and not inconsistent with this joint resolution nor contrary to the Constitution of the United States nor to any existing treaty of the United States, shall remain in force until the Congress of the United States shall otherwise determine.

Until legislation shall be enacted extending the United States customs laws and regulations to the Hawaiian Islands the existing customs relations of the Hawaiian Islands with the United States and other countries shall remain unchanged.

The public debt of the Republic of Hawaii, lawfully existing at the date of the passage of this joint resolution, including the amounts due to depositors in the Hawaiian Postal Savings Bank, is hereby assumed by the Government of the United States; but the liability of the United States in this regard shall in no case exceed four million dollars. So long, however, as the existing Government and the present commercial relations of the Hawaiian Islands are continued as hereinbefore, provided said Government shall continue to pay the interest on said debt.

There shall be no further immigration of Chinese into the Hawaiian Islands, except upon such conditions as are now or may hereafter be allowed by the laws of the United States; and no Chinese, by reason of anything herein contained, shall be allowed to enter the United States from the Hawaiian Islands.

Section One: The President shall appoint five commissioners, at least two of whom shall be residents of the Hawaiian Islands, who shall, as soon as reasonably practicable, recommend to Congress such legislation concerning the Hawaiian Islands as they shall deem necessary or proper.

Section Two: That the commissioners hereinbefore provided for shall be appointed by the President, by and with the advice and consent of the Senate.

Section Three: That the sum of one hundred thousand dollars, or so much thereof as may be necessary, is hereby appropriated, out of any money in the Treasury not otherwise appropriated, and to be immediately available, to be expended at the discretion of the President of the United States of America, for the purpose of carrying this joint resolution into effect.

Peace Treaty with Spain

During the Spanish-American War (1898), the United States lost 5,462 men in the four-month conflict, but only 379 in combat. The rest died from disease and other causes. Spain's casualties were much higher and, in addition, it lost the last of a once great New World empire.

Representatives of the United States and Spain met in Paris to arrange peace terms on October 1, 1898. In the final treaty, Spain gave up all claims to Cuba. It ceded Puerto Rico and the Pacific island of Guam to the United States. Spain also gave the Philippine Islands to the United States in exchange for $20 million. America had now become a colonial power.

The United States of America and Her Majesty the Queen Regent of Spain, in the name of her august son Don Alfonso XIII, desiring to end the state of war now existing between the two countries, have for that purpose appointed as plenipotentiaries:

The President of the United States,

William R. Day, Cushman K. Davis, William P. Frye, George Gray, and Whitelaw Reid, citizens of the United States;

And Her Majesty the Queen Regent of Spain,

Don Eugenio Montero Rios, president of the senate, Don Buenaventura de Abarzuza, senator of the Kingdom and ex-minister of the Crown; Don Jose de Garnica, deputy of the Cortes and associate justice of the supreme court; Don Wenceslao Ramirez de Villa-Urrutia, envoy extraordinary and minister plenipotentiary at Brussels, and Don Rafael Cerero, general of division;

Who, having assembled in Paris, and having exchanged their full powers, which were found to be in due and proper form, have, after discussion of the matters before them, agreed upon the following articles:

Article I

Spain relinquishes all claim of sovereignty over and title to Cuba.

And as the island is, upon its evacuation by Spain, to be occupied by the United States, the United States will, so long as such occupation shall last, assume and discharge the obligations that may under international law result from the fact of its occupation, for the protection of life and property.

Article II

Spain cedes to the United States the island of Puerto Rico and other islands now under Spanish sovereignty in the West Indies, and the island of Guam in the Marianas or Ladrones.

Article III

Spain cedes to the United States the archipelago known as the Philippine Islands, and comprehending the islands lying within the following line:

A line running from west to east along or near the twentieth parallel of north latitude, and through the middle of the navigable channel of Bachi, from the one hundred and eighteenth (118th) to the one hundred and twenty-seventh (127th) degree meridian of longitude east of Greenwich, thence along the one hundred and twenty seventh (127th) degree meridian of longitude east of Greenwich to the parallel of four degrees and forty five minutes (4° 45') north latitude, thence along the parallel of four degrees and forty five minutes (4° 45') north latitude to its intersection with the meridian of longitude one hundred and nineteen degrees and thirty five minutes (119° 35') east of Greenwich, thence

Theodore Roosevelt

Theodore Roosevelt had been assistant secretary of the navy under McKinley, but he resigned this position to take a commission with a cavalry unit during the Spanish-American War. Although second-in-command, the regiment soon was popularly known as Roosevelt's Rough Riders.

along the meridian of longitude one hundred and nineteen degrees and thirty five minutes (119° 35') east of Greenwich to the parallel of latitude seven degrees and forty minutes (7° 40') north, thence along the parallel of latitude of seven degrees and forty minutes (7° 40') north to its intersection with the one hundred and sixteenth (116th) degree meridian of longitude east of Greenwich, thence by a direct line to the intersection of the tenth (10th) degree parallel of north latitude with the one hundred and eighteenth (118th) degree meridian of longitude east of Greenwich, and thence along the one hundred and eighteenth (118th) degree meridian of longitude east of Greenwich to the point of beginning.

The United States will pay to Spain the sum of twenty million dollars ($20,000,000) within three months after the exchange of the ratifications of the present treaty.

Article IV

The United States will, for the term of ten years from the date of the exchange of the ratifications of the present treaty, admit Spanish ships and merchandise to the ports of the Philippine Islands on the same terms as ships and merchandise of the United States.

Article V

The United States will, upon the signature of the present treaty, send back to Spain, at its own cost, the Spanish soldiers taken as prisoners of war on the capture of Manila by the American forces. The arms of the soldiers in question shall be restored to them.

Spain will, upon the exchange of the ratifications of the present treaty, proceed to evacuate the Philippines, as well as the island of Guam, on terms similar to those agreed upon by the Commissioners appointed to arrange for the evacuation of Puerto Rico and other islands in the West Indies, under the Protocol of August 12, 1898, which is to continue in force till its provisions are completely executed.

The time within which the evacuation of the Philippine Islands and Guam shall be completed shall be fixed by the two Governments. Stands of colors, uncaptured war vessels, small arms, guns of all calibers, with their carriages and accessories, powder, ammunition, livestock, and materials and supplies of all kinds, belonging to the land and naval forces of Spain in the Philippines and Guam, remain the property of Spain. Pieces of heavy ordnance, exclusive of field artillery, in the fortifications and coast defenses, shall remain in their emplacements for the term of six months, to be reckoned from the exchange of ratifications of the treaty; and the United States may, in the meantime, purchase such material from Spain, if a satisfactory agreement between the two Governments on the subject shall be reached.

Article VI

Spain will, upon the signature of the present treaty, release all prisoners of war, and all persons detained or imprisoned for political offenses, in connection with the insurrections in Cuba and the Philippines and the war with the United States.

Reciprocally, the United States will release all persons made prisoners of war by the American forces, and will undertake to obtain the release of all Spanish prisoners in the hands of the insurgents in Cuba and the Philippines.

The Government of the United States will at its own cost return to Spain and the Government of Spain will at its own cost return to the United States, Cuba, Puerto Rico, and the Philippines, according to the situation of their respective homes, prisoners released or caused to be released by them, respectively, under this article.

Article VII

The United States and Spain mutually relinquish all claims for indemnity, national and individual, of every kind, of either Government, or of its citizens or subjects, against the other Government, that may have arisen since the beginning of the late insurrection in Cuba and prior to the exchange of ratifications of the present treaty, including all claims for indemnity for the cost of the war.

The United States will adjudicate and settle the claims of its citizens against Spain relinquished in this article.

Article VIII

In conformity with the provisions of Articles I, II, and III of this treaty, Spain relinquishes in Cuba, and cedes in Puerto Rico and other islands in the West Indies, in the island of Guam, and in the Philippine Archipelago, all the buildings, wharves, barracks, forts, structures, public highways and other immovable property which, in conformity with law, belong to the public domain, and as such belong to the Crown of Spain.

And it is hereby declared that the relinquishment or cession, as the case may be, to which the preceding paragraph refers, can not in any respect impair the property or rights which by law belong to the peaceful possession of property of all kinds, of provinces, municipalities, public or private establishments, ecclesiastical or civic bodies, or any other associations having legal capacity to acquire and possess property in the aforesaid territories renounced or ceded, or of private individuals, of whatsoever nationality such individuals may be.

The aforesaid relinquishment or cession, as the case may be, includes all

Castiron McKinley bootjack.

documents exclusively referring to the sovereignty relinquished or ceded that may exist in the archives of the Peninsula. Where any document in such archives only in part relates to said sovereignty, a copy of such part will be furnished whenever it shall be requested. Like rules shall be reciprocally observed in favor of Spain in respect of documents in the archives of the islands above referred to.

In the aforesaid relinquishment or cession, as the case may be, are also included such rights as the Crown of Spain and its authorities possess in respect of the official archives and records, executive as well as judicial, in the islands above referred to, which relate to said islands or the rights and property of their inhabitants. Such archives and records shall be carefully preserved, and private persons shall without distinction have the right to require, in accordance with law, authenticated copies of the contracts, wills and other instruments forming part of notorial protocols or files, or which may be contained in the executive or judicial archives, be the latter in Spain or in the islands aforesaid.

Article IX

Spanish subjects, natives of the Peninsula, residing in the territory over which Spain by the present treaty relinquishes or cedes her sovereignty, may remain in such territory or may remove therefrom, retaining in either event all their rights of property, including the right to sell or dispose of such property or of its proceeds; and they shall also have the right to carry on their industry, commerce and professions, being subject in respect thereof to such laws as are applicable to other foreigners. In case they remain in the territory they may preserve their allegiance to the Crown of Spain by making, before a court of record, within a year from the date of the exchange of ratifications of this treaty, a declaration of their decision to preserve such allegiance; in default of which declaration they shall be held to have renounced it and to have adopted the nationality of the territory in which they may reside.

The civil rights and political status of the native inhabitants of the territories hereby ceded to the United States shall be determined by the Congress.

Article X

The inhabitants of the territories over which Spain relinquishes or cedes her sovereignty shall be secured in the free exercise of their religion.

Article XI

The Spaniards residing in the territories over which Spain by this treaty cedes or relinquishes her sovereignty shall be subject in matters civil as well as criminal to the jurisdiction of the courts of the country wherein they reside, pursuant to the ordinary laws governing the same; and they shall have the right to appear before such courts, and to pursue the same course as citizens of the country to which the courts belong.

Article XII

Judicial proceedings pending at the time of the exchange of ratifications of this treaty in the territories over which Spain relinquishes or cedes her sovereignty shall be determined according to the following rules:

1. Judgments rendered either in civil suits between private individuals, or in criminal matters, before the date mentioned, and with respect to which there is no recourse or right of review under the Spanish law, shall be deemed to be final, and shall be executed in due form by competent authority in the territory within which such judgments should be carried out.

2. Civil suits between private individuals which may on the date mentioned be undetermined shall be prosecuted to judgment before the court in which they may then be pending or in the court that may be substituted therefor.

3. Criminal actions pending on the date mentioned before the Supreme Court of Spain against citizens of the territory which by this treaty ceases to

be Spanish shall continue under its jurisdiction until final judgment; but, such judgment having been rendered, the execution thereof shall be committed to the competent authority of the place in which the case arose.

Article XIII

The rights of property secured by copyrights and patents acquired by Spaniards in the Island of Cuba and in Puerto Rico, the Philippines and other ceded territories, at the time of the exchange of the ratifications of this treaty, shall continue to be respected. Spanish scientific, literary and artistic works, not subversive of public order in the territories in question, shall continue to be admitted free of duty into such territories, for the period of ten years, to be reckoned from the date of the exchange of the ratifications of this treaty.

Article XIV

Spain will have the power to establish consular officers in the ports and places of the territories, the sovereignty over which has been either relinquished or ceded by the present treaty.

Article XV

The Government of each country will, for the term of ten years, accord to the merchant vessels of the other country the same treatment in respect of all port charges, including entrance and clearance dues, light dues, and tonnage duties, as it accords to its own merchant vessels, not engaged in the coastwise trade.

Article XVI

It is understood that any obligations assumed in this treaty by the United States with respect to Cuba are limited to the time of its occupancy thereof; but it will upon termination of such occupancy, advise any Government established in the island to assume the same obligations.

Article XVII

The present treaty shall be ratified by the President of the United States, by and with the advice and consent of the Senate thereof, and by Her Majesty the Queen Regent of Spain; and the ratifications shall be exchanged at Washington within six months from the date hereof, or earlier if possible.

In faith whereof, we, the respective Plenipotentiaries, have signed this treaty and have hereunto affixed our seals.

Done in duplicate at Paris, the tenth day of December, in the year of Our Lord one thousand eight hundred and ninety-eight.

[Seal] William R. Day

[Seal] Cushman K. Davis

[Seal] William P. Frye

[Seal] Geo. Gray

[Seal] Whitelaw Reid

[Seal] Eugenio Montero Rios

[Seal] B. de Abarzuza

[Seal] J. de Garnica

[Seal] W. R. de Villa Urrutia

[Seal] Rafael Cerero

The Open Door Policy

In September 1899, Secretary of State John Hay sent notes to countries with treaty ports in China—England, France, Germany, and Japan. He asked them to keep their ports open to vessels of all nations on equal terms with equal tariffs on all imports and to charge equal railroad rates within their spheres of influence. Since none of these powers wished to state publicly that it intended to discriminate against the trade of other countries, none chose to dispute these points. Hay then announced that the "open door" had been "guaranteed." In the United States, he was credited with having won a great diplomatic victory. However, Hay's notes did not protect China from being cut up into spheres of influence where foreign powers had exclusive rights to build railroads and exploit the natural resources. Above all, Hay's well-publicized diplomacy popularized the expansionist aims of the McKinley administration.

Hay explained the "open door" policy in this excerpt from an 1899 letter to Andrew D. White who was the American delegate to the Hague Conference then conceptualizing the international court of arbitration.

At the time when the Government of the United States was informed by that of Germany that it had leased from His Majesty the Emperor of China the port of Kiao-chao and the adjacent territory in the province of Shantung, assurances were given to the ambassador of the United States at Berlin by the Imperial German minister for foreign affairs that the rights and privileges insured by treaties with China to citizens of the United States would not thereby suffer or be in anywise impaired within the area over which Germany had thus obtained control.

More recently, however, the British Government recognized by a formal agreement with Germany the exclusive right of the latter country to enjoy in said leased area and the contiguous "sphere of influence or interest" certain privileges, more especially those relating to railroads and mining enterprises; but, as the exact nature and extent of the rights thus recognized have not been clearly defined, it is possible that serious conflicts of interest may at any time arise, not only between British and German subjects within said area, but that the interests of our citizens may also be jeopardized thereby.

Earnestly desirous to remove any cause of irritation and to insure at the same time to the commerce of all nations in China the undoubted benefits which should accrue from a formal recognition by the various powers claiming "spheres of interest" that they shall enjoy perfect equality of treatment for their commerce and navigation within such "spheres," the Government of the United States would be pleased to see His German Majesty's Government give formal assurances and lend its cooperation in securing like assurances from the other interested powers that each within its respective sphere of whatever influence—

First. Will in no way interfere with any treaty port or any vested interest within any so-called "sphere of interest" or leased territory it may have in China.

Second. That the Chinese treaty tariff of the time being shall apply to all merchandise landed or shipped to all such ports as are within said "sphere of interest" (unless they be "free ports"), no matter to what nationality it may belong, and that duties so leviable shall be collected by the Chinese Government.

Third. That it will levy no higher harbor dues on vessels of another nationality frequenting any port in such "sphere" than shall be levied on vessels of its own nationality, and no higher railroad charges over lines built, controlled, or operated within its "sphere" on merchandise belonging to citizens or subjects of other nationalities transported through such "sphere" than shall be levied on similar merchandise belonging to its own nationals transported over equal distances.

The liberal policy pursued by His Imperial German Majesty in declaring Kiao-chao a free port and in aiding the Chinese Government in the establishment there of a customhouse are so clearly in line with the proposition which this Government is anxious to see recognized that it entertains the strongest hope that Germany will give its acceptance and hearty support.

The recent ukase of His Majesty the Emperor of Russia declaring the port of Ta-lien-wan open during the whole of the lease under which it is held from China, to the merchant ships of all nations, coupled with the categorical assurances made to this Government by His Imperial Majesty's representative at this capital at the time, and since repeated to me by the present Russian ambassador, seem to insure the support of the Emperor to the proposed measure. Our ambassador at the Court of St. Petersburg has, in consequence, been instructed to submit it to the Russian Government and to request their early consideration of it. A copy of my instruction on the subject to Mr. Tower is herewith inclosed for your confidential information.

The commercial interests of Great Britain and Japan will be so clearly served by the desired declaration of intentions, and the views of the govern-

John Hay (1838–1905) was Lincoln's private secretary, his biographer, and later Secretary of State under Presidents William McKinley and Theodore Roosevelt.

After Lincoln's election in 1860, John G. Nicolay, a journalist working as Lincoln's secretary, hired Hay, then a recent Brown University graduate. Together, they formed the most famous presidential staff of the nineteenth century. Nicolay and Hay, along with one assistant, screened visitors, sorted incoming mail, drafted routine correspondence and performed the office chores of Lincoln's White House. Hay recalled how often at night, Lincoln would wake him to laugh with him at some joke in the book the president was reading while vainly seeking sleep. The "Ancient" and the "Tycoon" were affectionate nicknames bestowed by Hay on his beloved chief. Daily contact with Lincoln during the more than four years of the Civil War gave the young man (for even in 1865 he was only twenty-seven years old) an abiding sense of the greatness of Lincoln. With Nicolay, Hay published *Abraham Lincoln: A History*, in ten volumes in 1890. More than one hundred years later, these volumes remain an invaluable record, based on original sources, of the Lincoln administration. In 1897, McKinley appointed him Secretary of State, an office he held until his death.

ments of these countries as to the desirability of the adoption of measures insuring the benefits of equality of treatment of all foreign trade throughout China are so similar to those entertained by the United States, that their acceptance of the propositions herein outlined and their cooperation in advocating their adoption by the other powers can be confidently expected.

The election of 1900 rematched the two candidates of the 1896 presidential election—Republican William McKinley and Democrat William Jennings Bryan. A major issue that the President faced was the selection of his running mate. Vice President Garret Hobart had died in November 1899. A clamor arose at once for the nomination of Governor Theodore Roosevelt of New York. Roosevelt had won fame in Cuba during the Spanish-American War of 1898. He also was very popular among younger Republicans, especially in the West. McKinley and his advisors considered Roosevelt immature and impetuous. But, they had no other candidate who aroused such enthusiasm. McKinley's victory by an even larger margin represented a popular endorsement of the Republican overseas expansion policies. "It is His will," maintained McKinley in defending the acquisition of an empire. McKinley carried every state except the "Solid South" and the four silver states of Colorado, Montana, Idaho, and Nevada. The Republican slogans of "Four years more of the Full Dinner Pail" and "Let Well Enough Alone" had prevailed.

The drizzle quickened to a downpour when, on March 4, 1901, William McKinley took his second oath of office. In a strong voice, he delivered his inaugural address.

When we assembled here on the 4th of March, 1897, there was great anxiety with regard to our currency and credit. None exists now. Then our Treasury receipts were inadequate to meet the current obligations of the Government. Now they are sufficient for all public needs, and we have a surplus instead of a deficit. Then I felt constrained to convene the Congress in extraordinary session to devise revenues to pay the ordinary expenses of the Government. Now I have the satisfaction to announce that the Congress just closed has reduced taxation in the sum of $41,000,000. Then there was deep solicitude because of the long depression in our manufacturing, mining, agricultural, and mercantile industries and the consequent distress of our laboring population. Now every avenue of production is crowded with activity, labor is well employed, and American products find good markets at home and abroad.

Our diversified productions, however, are increasing in such unprecedented volume as to admonish us of the necessity of still further enlarging our foreign markets by broader commercial relations. For this purpose reciprocal trade arrangements with other nations should in liberal spirit be carefully cultivated and promoted.

The national verdict of 1896 has for the most part been executed. Whatever remains unfulfilled is a continuing obligation resting with undiminished force upon the Executive and the Congress. But fortunate as our condition is, its permanence can only be assured by sound business methods and strict economy in national administration and legislation. We should not permit our great prosperity to lead us to reckless ventures in business or profligacy in public expenditures. While the Congress determines the objects and the sum of appropriations, the officials of the executive departments are responsible for honest and faithful disbursement, and it should be their constant care to avoid waste and extravagance.

Honesty, capacity, and industry are nowhere more indispensable than in public employment. These should be fundamental requisites to original appointment and the surest guaranties against removal.

Four years ago we stood on the brink of war without the people knowing it and without any preparation or effort at preparation for the impending peril.

(Above) Photograph of a group of young women showing their support for Bryan. They wear a variety of campaign buttons, badges, and bandannas. (Opposite) A variety of Bryan campaign memorabilia from the 1900 election, including celluloid buttons, a ribbon with an interesting slogan, and a 1900 poster that depicts Bryan as an apostle of free silver and an opponent of imperialism. On the lower part of the poster the Trust octopus is engulfing American farms and factories.

In his second election, Bryan garnered fewer electoral votes (155) than he had in 1896 (172), while his percentage of the popular vote fell from 47.7 percent to 45.5 percent. However, he solidified his stature as one of the most important political leaders in American history, and set the terms of public discourse for years to come.

I did all that in honor could be done to avert the war, but without avail. It became inevitable; and the Congress at its first regular session, without party division, provided money in anticipation of the crisis and in preparation to meet it. It came. The result was signally favorable to American arms and in the highest degree honorable to the Government. It imposed upon us obligations from which we cannot escape and from which it would be dishonorable to seek escape. We are now at peace with the world, and it is my fervent prayer that if differences arise between us and other powers they may be settled by peaceful arbitration and that hereafter we may be spared the horrors of war.

Intrusted by the people for a second time with the office of President, I enter upon its administration appreciating the great responsibilities which attach to this renewed honor and commission, promising unreserved devotion on my part to their faithful discharge and reverently invoking for my guidance the direction and favor of Almighty God. I should shrink from the duties this day assumed if I did not feel that in their performance I should have the co-operation of the wise and patriotic men of all parties. It encourages me for the great task which I now undertake to believe that those who voluntarily committed to me the trust imposed upon the Chief Executive of the Republic will give to me generous support in my duties to "preserve, protect, and defend, the Constitution of the United States" and to "care that the laws be faithfully executed." The national purpose is indicated through a national election. It is the constitutional method of ascertaining the public will. When once it is registered it is a law to us all, and faithful observance should follow its decrees.

Strong hearts and helpful hands are needed, and, fortunately, we have them in every part of our beloved country. We are reunited. Sectionalism has disappeared. Division on public questions can no longer be traced by the war maps of 1861. These old differences less and less disturb the judgment. Existing problems demand the thought and quicken the conscience of the country, and the responsibility for their presence, as well as for their righteous settlement, rests upon us all—no more upon me than upon you. There are some national questions in the solution of which patriotism should exclude partisanship. Magnifying their difficulties will not take them off our hands nor facilitate their adjustment. Distrust of the capacity, integrity, and high purposes of the American people will not be an inspiring theme for future political contests. Dark pictures and gloomy forebodings are worse than useless. These only becloud, they do not help to point the way of safety and honor. "Hope maketh not ashamed." The prophets of evil were not the builders of the Republic, nor in its crises since have they saved or served it. The faith of the fathers was a mighty force in its creation, and the faith of their descendants has wrought its progress and furnished its defenders. They are obstructionists who despair, and who would destroy confidence in the ability of our people to solve wisely and for civilization the mighty problems resting upon them. The American people, intrenched in freedom at home, take their love for it with them wherever they go, and they reject as mistaken and unworthy the doctrine that we lose our own liberties by securing the enduring foundations of liberty to others. Our institutions will not deteriorate by extension, and our sense of justice will not abate under tropic suns in distant seas. As heretofore, so hereafter will the nation demonstrate its fitness to administer any new estate which events devolve upon it, and in the fear of God will "take occasion by the hand and make the bounds of freedom wider yet." If there are those among us who would make our way more difficult, we must not be disheartened, but the more earnestly dedicate ourselves to the task upon which we have rightly entered. The path of progress is seldom smooth. New things are often found hard to do. Our fathers found them so. We find them so. They are inconvenient. They cost us something. But are we not made better for the effort and sacrifice, and are not those we serve lifted up and blessed?

We will be consoled, too, with the fact that opposition has confronted every onward movement of the Republic from its opening hour until now, but without success. The Republic has marched on and on, and its step has exalted freedom and humanity. We are undergoing the same ordeal as did our prede-

A 1900 campaign poster contrasting economic desolation, fiscal chaos, and Spanish tyranny in Cuba under the Democrats with American prosperity and Cuban liberty under McKinley.

cessors nearly a century ago. We are following the course they blazed. They triumphed. Will their successors falter and plead organic impotency in the nation? Surely after 125 years of achievement for mankind we will not now surrender our equality with other powers on matters fundamental and essential to nationality. With no such purpose was the nation created. In no such spirit has it developed its full and independent sovereignty. We adhere to the principle of equality among ourselves, and by no act of ours will we assign to ourselves a subordinate rank in the family of nations.

My fellow-citizens, the public events of the past four years have gone into history. They are too near to justify recital. Some of them were unforeseen; many of them momentous and far-reaching in their consequences to ourselves and our relations with the rest of the world. The part which the United States bore so honorably in the thrilling scenes in China, while new to American life, has been in harmony with its true spirit and best traditions, and in dealing with the results its policy will be that of moderation and fairness.

We face at this moment a most important question that of the future relations of the United States and Cuba. With our near neighbors we must remain close friends. The declaration of the purposes of this Government in the resolution of April 20, 1898, must be made good. Ever since the evacuation of the island by the army of Spain, the Executive, with all practicable speed, has been assisting its people in the successive steps necessary to the establishment of a free and independent government prepared to assume and perform the obligations of international law which now rest upon the United States under the treaty of Paris. The convention elected by the people to frame a constitution is approaching the completion of its labors. The transfer of American control to the new government is of such great importance, involving an obligation resulting from our intervention and the treaty of peace, that I am glad to be advised by the recent act of Congress of the policy which the legislative branch of the Government deems essential to the best interests of Cuba and the United States. The principles which led to our intervention require that the fundamental law upon which the new government rests should be adapted to secure a government capable of performing the duties and discharging the functions of a separate nation, of observing its international obligations of protecting life and property, insuring order, safety, and liberty, and conforming to the established and historical policy of the United States in its relation to Cuba.

The peace which we are pledged to leave to the Cuban people must carry with it the guaranties of permanence. We became sponsors for the pacification of the island, and we remain accountable to the Cubans, no less than to our own country and people, for the reconstruction of Cuba as a free commonwealth on abiding foundations of right, justice, liberty, and assured order. Our enfranchisement of the people will not be completed until free Cuba shall "be a reality, not a name; a perfect entity, not a hasty experiment bearing within itself the elements of failure."

While the treaty of peace with Spain was ratified on the 6th of February, 1899, and ratifications were exchanged nearly two years ago, the Congress has indicated no form of government for the Philippine Islands. It has, however, provided an army to enable the Executive to suppress insurrection, restore peace, give security to the inhabitants, and establish the authority of the United States throughout the archipelago. It has authorized the organization of native troops as auxiliary to the regular force. It has been advised from time to time of the acts of the military and naval officers in the islands, of my action in appointing civil commissions, of the instructions with which they were charged, of their duties and powers, of their recommendations, and of their several acts under executive commission, together with the very complete general information they have submitted. These reports fully set forth the conditions, past and present, in the islands, and the instructions clearly show the principles which will guide the Executive until the Congress shall, as it is required to do by the treaty, determine "the civil rights and political status of the native inhabitants." The Congress having added the sanction of its authority to the powers already possessed and exercised by the Executive under the Constitution, thereby leaving with the Executive the responsibility for the government of the Philippines, I shall continue the efforts already begun until order shall be restored throughout the islands, and as fast as conditions permit will establish local governments, in the formation of which the full co-operation of the people has been already invited, and when established will encourage the people to administer them. The settled purpose, long ago proclaimed, to afford the inhabitants of the islands self-government as fast as they were ready for it will be pursued with earnestness and fidelity. Already something has been accomplished in this direction. The Government's representatives, civil and military, are doing faithful and noble work in their mission of emancipation and merit the approval and support of their countrymen. The most liberal terms of amnesty have already been communicated to the insurgents, and the way is still open for those who have raised their arms against the Government for honorable submission to its authority. Our countrymen should not be deceived. We are not waging war against the inhabitants of the Philippine Islands. A portion of them are making war against the United States. By far the greater part of the inhabitants recognize American sovereignty and welcome it as a guaranty of order and of security for life, property, liberty, freedom of conscience, and the pursuit of happiness. To them full protection will be given. They shall not be abandoned. We will not leave the destiny of the loyal millions the islands to the disloyal thousands who are in rebellion against the United States. Order under civil institutions will come as soon as those who now break the peace shall keep it. Force will not be needed or used when those who make war against us shall make it no more. May it end without further bloodshed, and there be ushered in the reign of peace to be made permanent by a government of liberty under law!

Glass canteen with a rope handle, picturing the 1900 Republican candidates, McKinley and Roosevelt. In the words of historian John Milton Cooper jr., "When the voters went to the polls on November 6, continuity and majority contentment prevailed ... A popular president with a fresh new face for a running mate enjoyed all the advantages of incumbency, a largely prosperous economy, and the afterglow of easy victory in what his secretary of state called "a splendid little war."

★ The Assassination of McKinley ★

absolute acquiescence in
the vital principle of rep
but to force, the vital pr
despotism....a well-discipl
peace, and for the first m
relieve them....the supre
authority....economy
be lightly burden
and ...ered pres
of agricui·ure,
fusion of inform
bar of the public

rear, that this government,
...is a best hope, may, by possibility, want energy
to preserve itself?....I trust not....I believe this, on the
contrary, the strongest government on earth....I believe
it the only one, where every man, at the call of the law,
would fly to the standard of the law, and would meet in-
vasions of the public order as his own personal concern,
Sometimes it is said, that man cannot be trusted with
the government of himself. Can he then be trusted w
the government of others? Or have we found angels
the form of kings, to govern him? Let history ans

My   'ote for

McKinley had innovative goals for his second term. He planned to break precedent by traveling to Cuba or Puerto Rico. He intended to engage the trust issue more directly. He also had given thought to replacing the high protective tariff with a series of reciprocal trade treaties. But, on September 6, 1901, he was shot while on a receiving line at the Pan-American Exposition in Buffalo, New York. The president died of his wounds eight days later.

The following description of the assassination was published in the Buffalo *Courier* on September 7, 1901. It remains the best firsthand account of the tragic event.

President McKinley Shot at Public reception in the Temple of Music

---

One Bullet Passed Through Stomach —Wound Critical—Not Fatal

Raging Mobs attempt to lynch anarchist— sixty-fifth regiment is under waiting orders

---

"I did my duty," exclaims the assassin, who says he is a disciple of Emma Goldman

---

While extending in friendly greeting his hand of fellowship, in the Temple of Music at the Pan-American Exposition, William McKinley, President of the United States, was shot down at the hands of either an Anarchist or a lunatic, a few minutes after 4 o'clock yesterday afternoon.

The assassin was captured and is safely in custody, while the President has undergone an operation and is at the home of President Milburn of the Pan-American Exposition, whose guest he has been. Grave fears are entertained as to his recovery, the second bullet having entered the abdomen, completely penetrating the stomach. It has not been found and further search for it has been abandoned for the present. The first bullet struck the breast and did not penetrate. When Mrs. McKinley was told of the tragedy she was at the home of Mr. Milburn and it was reported that she bore up well although still an invalid.

THE WORLD'S ANXIETY

The world is pouring its messages of regret into the doorway of the Milburn home. Thousands of telegrams have been received, and an effort

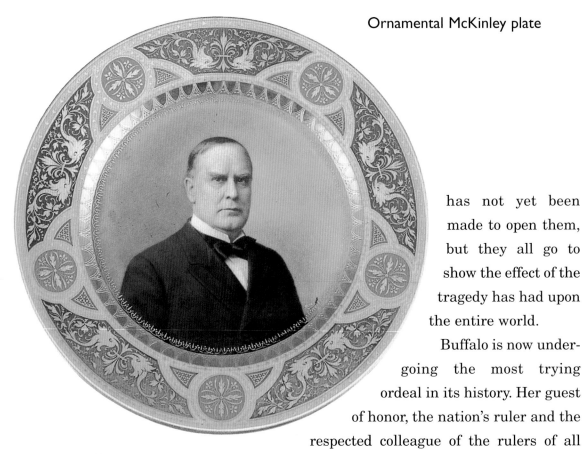

Ornamental McKinley plate

has not yet been made to open them, but they all go to show the effect of the tragedy has had upon the entire world.

Buffalo is now undergoing the most trying ordeal in its history. Her guest of honor, the nation's ruler and the respected colleague of the rulers of all civilized nations, lies between life and death within her own doors. No adequate description may be attempted of the impression this tragedy has made upon the people of Buffalo. Everywhere people are so horrified that the crime is discussed in the shortest sentences, and many are the expressions of revenge.

MILITIA ON WAITING ORDERS

Exciting mobs have gathered about the 1st Precinct Police Station, wherein the assassin is a prisoner, and the police have been kept busy all night dispersing them. Fearing the worst might come, the militia had been ordered into readiness. Governor Odell has arrived and the 65th Regiment is under waiting orders. A few minutes after the President was shot, the Midway closed and last night the entire Exposition grounds were in darkness and deserted.

ASSASSIN'S CONFESSION

The assassin, in a confession made to the District Attorney, court officials and the police at midnight, said that his name was Leon Czolgosz, that he was 28 years old, a blacksmith, and that he had come to Buffalo from from his home in Cleveland three days ago with the express intention of assassinating the President. He said he had been a student of Emma Goldman, the Anarchist, had approved her doctrines and did not believe in this form of government. He described with accuracy and with seeming pride the preparations he had made to kill the President, how he had practiced in folding the handkerchief about his hand so as to conceal the revolver, and described how he had shot the President.

To a *Courier* reporter District Attorney Penney gave the substance of Czolgosz's confession as follows:

"This man has admitted shooting the President. He says he intended to kill; that he has been planning to do it for the last three days since he came here. He went into the Temple of Music with murder in his heart, intending to shoot to kill. He fixed up his hand by tying a handkerchief around it and waited his turn to get near the President, just as the newspapers have described. When he got directly in front of the President he fired. He says he had no confederates, that he was entirely alone in the planning and execution of his diabolical act."

This in substance is the confession made by Czolgosz, who is a German-Pole and says his home is in the vicinity of Cleveland, Ohio. He is 28 years old, unmarried, and has seven brothers and two sisters living there. He worked for a time in the wire mills at Newark, Ohio. He exhibits no signs of contrition

Glass tumbler with acid-etched portraits of McKinley and Roosevelt.

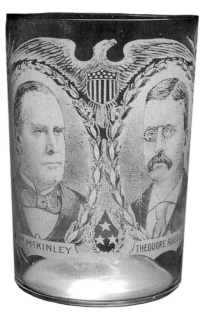

With the assassination of William McKinley in September 1901, Theodore Roosevelt, not quite forty-three, became the youngest and one of the most colorful presidents of the United States. Rancher, soldier, naturalist, scholar, plus a dozen other things, Roosevelt had achieved national fame during the Spanish-American War. His reputation was sufficient to elect him governor of New York in 1898. In 1900, the New York Republican bosses wished to have this dynamic man out of state politics so they pushed him for the vice presidential nomination. Within six months of his election to this secondary post, he was suddenly elevated to the highest office in the land. The days of the post-Civil War sedentary and docile presidents had ended. Roosevelt, with his inexhaustible energy and tremendous personal magnetism, was bound to arouse greater interest and greater antagonism than his predecessors.

and acts as if he had done a praiseworthy, instead of a dastardly, act.

The President, with Mrs. McKinley, had been to Niagara Falls up until 3:30 o'clock, when his special train brought them to the Exposition. There, Mrs. McKinley took a carriage to the Milburn home, she feeling fatigued. The President and his party were driven to the Government building, where a light lunch was served, and then the President, accompanied only by President Milburn, Secretary Cortelyou and the Secret Service men, drove to the Temple of Music, where it had been arranged to have a public reception.

NUMEROUS SOLDIERS

The President had taken his position under a bower of palms, and to his left was President Milburn, to his right Secretary Cortelyou, and opposite them Secret Service operatives Ireland and Foster. They were so arranged that the crowd would have to pass in single file. Along the aisle down which the public must pass were numerous soldiers from the 73d Sea Coast Artillery and guards from the Exposition police.

The President was never in a better mood; he was smiling from the moment he stepped into the building, and when he announced that he was ready for the doors to be thrown open, he appeared as though the coming onslaught of handshaking was to be a long-looked-for pleasure.

MUSIC OF THE ORGAN

Two hundred people had not passed the President when the tragedy which was to startle the world turned the joyous scene into one of indestructible excitement, assault and pandemonium. Organist Gomph had reached the highest notes in one of Bach's masterpieces on the great pipe organ, and as he stopped at the height to let the strains reverberate through the auditorium the two shots rang out.

Further READING

GENERAL REFERENCE

Israel, Fred L. *Student's Atlas of American Presidential Elections, 1789–1996*. Washington, D.C.: Congressional Quarterly Books, 1998.

Levy, Peter B., editor. *100 Key Documents in American History*. Westport, Conn.: Praeger, 1999.

Mieczkowski, Yarek. *The Routledge Historical Atlas of Presidential Elections*. New York: Routledge, 2001.

Polsby, Nelson W., and Aaron Wildavsky. *Presidential Elections: Strategies and Structures of American Politics*. 10th edition. New York: Chatham House, 2000.

Watts, J. F., and Fred L. Israel, editors. *Presidential Documents*. New York: Routledge, 2000.

Widmer, Ted. *The New York Times Campaigns: A Century of Presidential Races*. New York: DK Publishing, 2000.

POLITICAL AMERICANA REFERENCE

Cunningham, Noble E. Jr. *Popular Images of the Presidency: From Washington to Lincoln*. Columbia: University of Missouri Press, 1991.

Melder, Keith. *Hail to the Candidate: Presidential Campaigns from Banners to Broadcasts*. Washington, D.C.: Smithsonian Institution Press, 1992.

Schlesinger, Arthur M. jr., Fred L. Israel, and David J. Frent. *Running for President: The Candidates and their Images*. 2 vols. New York: Simon and Schuster, 1994.

Warda, Mark. *100 Years of Political Campaign Collectibles*. Clearwater, Fla.: Galt Press, 1996.

THE ELECTION OF 1896
and the Administration of William McKinley

Allen, Robert A. *William Jennings Bryan: Golden-Tongued Orator*. Fenton, Mich.: Mott Media, 1992.

Armstrong, William H. *Major McKinley: William McKinley and the Civil War*. Ashland, Ohio: Kent State University Press, 2000.

Brands, H. W. *T.R.: The Last Romantic*. New York: Basic Books, 1998.

Damiani, Brian P. *Advocates of Empire: William McKinley, the Senate and American Expansion, 1898–1899*. New York: Garland, 1987.

Glad, Paul W. *McKinley, Bryan, and the People*. Chicago: Ivan R. Dee, 1991.

Gould, Lewis L. *The Presidency of William McKinley*. Lawrence: University Press of Kansas, 1981.

————. *The Spanish-American War and President McKinley*. Lawrence: University Press of Kansas, 1982.

Kent, Zachary. *William McKinley*. New York: Children's Press, 1988.

McKinley, William. *The Speeches and Addresses of William McKinley from March 1, 1897, to May 30, 1900*. New York: Best Books, 2000.

Morris, Edmund. *Theodore Rex*. New York: Random House, 2001.

Trask, David F. *The War with Spain in 1898*. Lincoln: University of Nebraska Press, 1997.

Wilson, Antoine. *The Assassination of William McKinley*. New York: Rosen, 2002.

Zimmermann, Warren. *First Great Triumph: How Five Americans Made Their Country a World Power*. New York: Farrar Straus & Giroux, 2002.

INDEX

Numbers in **bold italics** refer to captions.

The EDITORS

ARTHUR M. SCHLESINGER JR. holds the Albert Schweitzer Chair in the Humanities at the Graduate Center of the City University of New York. He is the author of more than a dozen books, including *The Age of Jackson*; *The Vital Center*; *The Age of Roosevelt* (3 vols.); *A Thousand Days: John F. Kennedy in the White House*; *Robert Kennedy and His Times*; *The Cycles of American History*; and *The Imperial Presidency*. Professor Schlesinger served as Special Assistant to President Kennedy (1961–63). His numerous awards include: the Pulitzer Prize for History; the Pulitzer Prize for Biography; two National Book Awards; The Bancroft Prize; and the American Academy of Arts and Letters Gold Medal for History.

FRED L. ISRAEL is professor emeritus of American history, City College of New York. He is the author of *Nevada's Key Pittman* and has edited *The War Diary of Breckinridge Long* and *Major Peace Treaties of Modern History, 1648–1975* (5 vols.) He holds the Scribe's Award from the American Bar Association for his joint editorship of the *Justices of the United States Supreme Court* (4 vols.). For more than 25 years Professor Israel has compiled and edited the Gallup Poll into annual reference volumes.

DAVID J. FRENT is the president of Political Americana Auctions, Oakhurst, NJ. With his wife, Janice, he has assembled the nation's foremost private collection of political campaign memorabilia. Mr. Frent has designed exhibits for corporations, the Smithsonian Institution, and the United States Information Agency. A member of the board of directors of the American Political Items Collectors since 1972, he was elected to its Hall of Fame for his "outstanding contribution to preserving and studying our political heritage."